BX   Breault, William.
4483.8
.B74   The lady from
1986   Dublin

THE
LADY
FROM
DUBLIN

THE
LADY
FROM
DUBLIN

WRITTEN AND
ILLUSTRATED BY

WILLIAM BREAULT, SJ

QUINLAN PRESS
Boston

Published by Quinlan Press
131 Beverly Street
Boston, MA 02114

Library of Congress Cataloging-in-Publication Data

Breault, William.
    The lady from Dublin

    Bibliography: p.
    1. McAuley, Catherine, 1786-1841.   2. Nuns—
Ireland—Biography.   3. Sisters of Mercy—History—
19th century.   I. Title.
BX4483.8.B74   1986   271'.92'024   [B]   85-62496
ISBN 0-933341-16-4

Printed in the United States of America,
September 1986

I wish to dedicate this book to Kathleen Dunne, one of the thousands of contemporary followers of the lady from Dublin, Catherine McAuley. Without Kathleen's help and steady encouragement this book would not have been written.

CONTENTS

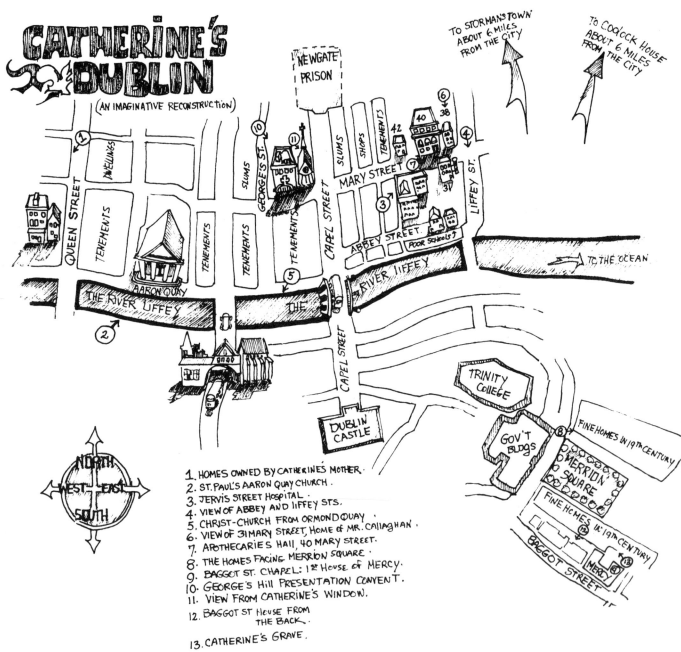

CATHERINE'S DUBLIN

(AN IMAGINATIVE RECONSTRUCTION)

TO STORMAN'S TOWN
ABOUT 6 MILES
FROM THE CITY

TO COOLOCK HOUSE
ABOUT 6 MILES
FROM THE CITY

NEWGATE PRISON

SLUMS

SHOPS

TENEMENTS

42

40

38

MARY STREET

GEORGE'S ST.

SLUMS

TENEMENTS

CAPEL STREET

31

ABBEY STREET.

LIFFEY ST.

POOR SCHOOLS

QUEEN STREET

DWELLINGS

TENEMENTS

TENEMENTS

TENEMENTS

TENEMENTS

TENEMENTS

AARON QUAY

THE RIVER LIFFEY

THE RIVER LIFFEY

THE

RIVER LIFFEY

TO THE OCEAN

CAPEL STREET

TRINITY COLLEGE

GOV'T BLDGS

FINE HOMES IN 19TH CENTURY

MERRION SQUARE

FINE HOMES IN 19TH CENTURY

BAGGOT STREET

MERCY

DUBLIN CASTLE

NORTH
WEST — EAST
SOUTH

1. HOMES OWNED BY CATHERINE'S MOTHER.
2. ST. PAUL'S AARON QUAY CHURCH.
3. JERVIS STREET HOSPITAL.
4. VIEW OF ABBEY AND LIFFEY STS.
5. CHRIST-CHURCH FROM ORMOND QUAY.
6. VIEW OF 31 MARY STREET, HOME OF MR. CALLAGHAN.
7. APOTHECARIES HALL, 40 MARY STREET.
8. THE HOMES FACING MERRION SQUARE.
9. BAGGOT ST. CHAPEL: 1ST HOUSE OF MERCY.
10. GEORGE'S HILL PRESENTATION CONVENT.
11. VIEW FROM CATHERINE'S WINDOW.
12. BAGGOT ST HOUSE FROM THE BACK.

13. CATHERINE'S GRAVE.

 # Chapter I

Dublin Town

The passport official at Dublin Airport, noticing the occupation I had written on the arrival form—priest/writer—looked at me, hesitated, then said, "How long are you going to stay?"

"About thirty days," I answered. He checked me through.

Outside the air terminal, an old lemon and cream colored bus wheezed and clanked to the curbing. It was half-filled with people, all of whom stopped talking and stared once I got on and asked for directions.

"I'd like to get off at the Cat and Cage Pub." There were more stares. I sat down and pulled my suitcases up on the seat beside me. It was obvious to everyone on the bus that I was an American. Outside, the gray mist had turned to rain.

Jolting along in the ancient vehicle, I thought, "Where do I start? How do I find some trace of Catherine McAuley, a woman who lived a hundred and thirty years ago?"

I got off at the Cat and Cage Pub on the outskirts of Dublin and followed a brick street with a twelve-foot wall on the left and tight, neat houses on the right until I reached All Hallows College, where I was going to stay. In the center of vast stretches of green lawn stood an array of buildings clustered around the first home built on this property in 1725. Now, 250 years later, the college was to be my home for the next month.

I was met at the door by a tall, vigorous man dressed in black. He showed me to my room, four stories up, while filling me with historical details of the college, one of which caught my ear: the college was built on land leased from the famous Irish patriot, Daniel O'Connell, a friend of the woman I was looking for.

That night I put my first impressions of the city of Dublin down on paper, and I recalled what little I knew of Catherine McAuley. She was born in

Drumcondra Road on the way to Belfast

Dublin in 1786 and died here in 1841. A single woman, she lived an obscure life for forty years, then inherited a fortune that changed her life. With the money, she built a large home for the poor on Baggot Street, on the south side of Dublin. That house became the birthplace for the largest order of English-speaking religious women in the world, the Sisters of Mercy.

I woke the next morning with the same thought I had earlier: "Where do I start?" The obvious place to start my search was at the home Catherine had built for the poor. From the women who still lived in that house, her followers, I hoped to discover something about her birthplace and early life.

That afternoon I boarded a bus going toward the center of the city. I glanced at the name of the road: Drumcondra Road, leading from Dublin to Belfast. As the bus took me into Dublin, I looked at the city: soot-covered buildings, some dating back hundreds of years; chimney pots, domes and spires punctuating the horizon. The people walking the streets and sitting with me on the bus were dressed in neutral grays. Very little color.

At the main thoroughfare, O'Connell Street, I got off and queued up for the southbound transfer. My eyes swept the crowded boulevard: cars, buses and people in a constant state of motion. Rising above all the traffic was the statue of the nineteenth century Irish patriot, Daniel O'Connell. Angels, great men of history and other famous liberators formed the base of the statue, but towering over them all was O'Connell, a scroll in his right hand, the symbol of his profession, law. His left hand was tucked inside his shirt front in the Napoleonic manner.

This was the man on whose land I was temporarily living. His statue stands firmly in the center of Dublin's main street, named after him. His contribution to Ireland is just as firmly rooted in her history, for he had worked tirelessly for twenty-nine years to achieve emancipation for Ireland's six million Catholics. And he had known and admired the woman for whom I was looking, Catherine McAuley, because of her work with the sick and the poor.

While I was looking at the "Liberator," with his strong head and lanternlike jaw, the southbound bus pulled up to the curb. Once the bus crossed the bridge and the River Liffey, the Dublin scene changed: gone were the old tenement buildings, the open markets with vegetable stalls and the crowded, quite ordinary department stores. South of the river I discovered the posh shops of Grafton Street, the government buildings of the Republic, museums, art galleries and miles of fine Georgian homes. Dublin, it seemed, was not one city, but two: north and south, divided by the river.

I got off at Leeson Street and, after a four-block walk, came to the home that Catherine had built for the poor in 1827, gray, three stories high and surrounded by a black, spiked fence. I pressed the doorbell and waited. Since I wasn't dressed as a priest—an automatic passe-partout to everything Catholic in Catholic Ireland—I had prepared a short introduction.

The door opened tentatively. Sister Finian, the superior of the house, narrowed her eyes: "Yes?"

This wasn't much of an invitation to converse, so I began my rehearsed opening: "Sister, I'm a priest from the United States. I would like to find out something about—" I got no further. The door was opened wide, tea was set, and we began talking.

Later that afternoon, we sat in the room where Catherine had died. I had already been given a picture of the house in which she was born, so I made a sketch of it. "Where is the original site of Catherine's birthplace," I asked Sister, "and how to I get there?"

"Retrace your steps," she said, "to the north side of the river, up and out of the center of town. Dublin is like a saucer with the city in the very center, so you'll be driving away from the center to the higher, surrounding rim of soft, green, rolling hills. In those hills is a place called Stormanstown. That is where Catherine McAuley was born in 1786."

O'Connell Street, Dublin

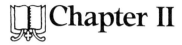 # Chapter II

The Lady's Birthplace: Stormanstown

The next day, on the way to Catherine's birthplace, I got into a conversation with a young Irishman sitting next to me. "Is it true," I asked, "that not long ago there were only two classes of people in Ireland, clergy and laity?"

"Oh yes," he answered. "In fact, that's still true today. It's as if the priests belong to a special caste, high above the people. But it wasn't too long ago that a person had to get off a path and stand aside whenever he saw a priest coming."

Then he asked me what America was like, and finally, what I did for a living. I told him I was a priest. His eyes blinked a few times, then opened wide.

"Well," he said, eyeing my backpack, "what are you doing over here? Visiting? Or making a tour of the country?"

"I'm doing some sketching." Again the eyes opened wide. "But the main reason I'm here is to find out what I can about the foundress of the Sisters of Mercy."

"Oh, Catherine McAuley?"

"Yes," I said.

"But why her?"

"Well, to tell you the truth, I like her. She seems to have been down-to-earth. I think she had a fine sense of humor. Anyone who was a foundress of a religious order and could call herself "Kitty" must have been an interesting woman. Most founders and foundresses seem quite strict to me."

The young man looked around at the people on the bus—perhaps looking for a Sister of Mercy—and said, "Well, the Sisters of Mercy seem strict to me. In fact, almost all sisters and priests seem that way."

"Perhaps they are," I answered, "but if you read this woman's letters I think you'd find she was a very warm-hearted person."

He looked at me with a question, but it never reached his lips. Since my stop

Stormanstown House

was coming up, I said goodbye and left him sitting in the back seat, probably wondering about priests and nuns.

I got off the bus and walked to the supposed site of Catherine's birth: a parking lot. From there I looked back and down on the city next to the sea. The sky was dark and overcast. A sharp wind blew. I turned my back to the sea and looked uphill to row upon row of high-rise dwellings for the poor—crowded, low-rent apartments, literally stuffed with people.

Behind each apartment, waiting for the sun to dry them, shirts, pants and other clothes were strung along makeshift clotheslines: so many clothes, in fact, that they seemed to be a part of the architectural design. I found out later that families were so crowded together in these flats that they contained ''the highest density of children in all of Europe.''

The women of these flats had a harried look about them, with lines of self-defense around the corners of their eyes and mouth. Despite the spacious, green, manicured lawns surrounding the flats, there was little or no privacy. No one owned a yard. And the flats themselves did not seem to qualify as private property. Four-letter words decorated the walls lining the nearby highway; cars sped by. The drab, wet laundry flapped in the moist ocean breeze. Ten or eleven children recently returned from school were scratching on the damp walls, fighting and forming gangs. They were playing with an abandoned shopping cart in the shadows of the huge buildings, near puddles of water that never quite got enough sun to dry up.

Up close, the wind shrieked around the sharp edges of the apartments. The children who were playing didn't seem to have any other goal than to kill time or stay out of the apartments: the beginnings of a ghetto.

I could see the ignorance, idleness and overcrowding that cause a ghetto. Aware of the same phenomenon in her own time, Catherine had built her home and schools for the poor. In a flyer sent out to solicit funds for it, she revealed what she was trying to alleviate:

In these schools five hundred poor girls may daily experience the blessing of religious instruction and being practiced in various branches of industry come forward shielded from all the evils incident to ignorance and idleness, prepared as Christians to discharge the duties of the state in life to which it has pleased God to call them.

The irony of her birthplace becoming a ghetto struck me full force.

Catherine McAuley was born here in 1786, give or take a few years—no one really knows since there are no records of her baptism or birth. In the words of a contemporary of Catherine: "It may be that the children were baptized in their home and the priest failed to make an entry in the church register of his giving them the sacrament."

Catherine's father, James McAuley, married a much younger woman, Eleanor Conway. They had three children, Catherine, Mary and James. Aside from that, not much is known about their father: "Still missing are birth, date of death, and place of burial of James McAuley."

Standing just off the highway, which was a narrow dirt road in Catherine's time, I did a sketch of the flats, then returned to All Hallows College.

For the next few days I stayed within walking distance of the college. I made new plans, worked on some sketches and wrote in my diary. In the evenings I walked the paths around the college, listening to the bells of the city and smelling the omnipresent diesel fumes. Gradually, my experience of the sights and sounds of Dublin worked their way into a kind of poem:

Dublin: an impression
Pub
per block
on block
of brick,
arched-over
Georgian
with Ionic columns
standing smooth sentry
to solid paneled doors,
opened
with brass knobs
burnished
daily;
massive
gray
Periclean buildings
hedged and fenced
with iron spikes
and walls topped

13

Stormanstown today

with broken glass.
And the sounds
of thick, high-heeled
shoes
clopping
or metal taps;
grunts,
sharp hisses
and airy exhalations
of the multi-decked buses,
weaving
a perilous way
through history,
entombed.
On the horizon,
brick chimney pots
exhausting
grayness
into the sky,
condensing
into a fine mist
over the G.P.O.
still showing
her battle scars
from revolution!
A meat and potato people
with fierce loyalties:
the faith,
patriotism
bread,
football,
and tea.

While praying outside one evening, I met Kevin, a kind of twentieth century hermit, with wild unmanageable hair, mustache and beard. His shoes were worn through and his clothes were shabby. In his arms he carried old bags, books and I don't know what else. He was wearing a long, dark green coat.

Since it was almost dark, I hadn't noticed him at first. I was walking back and forth in front of a Gothic chapel when he stopped me:

"Excuse me? Would you have the time?"

I stopped only briefly and said, "Yes. Nine thirty." The fewer the words, the less the chance he could tell where I was from—that would avoid a long conversation.

"Would you be from Dublin?"

"No," I responded, laughing inwardly at the idea of being mistaken for a Dubliner.

"Canada, perhaps?"

"No," I said, "America."

"Ahh . . . America!" Then he began a conversation unlike any I have ever experienced. Kevin talked and talked, but only of Christ, Mary, the Holy Sacrifice of the Mass, of the many priests he knew around Dublin and of his family, especially his sister who had suffocated recently in a London fire. Would I pray for her? And as we talked, crossing and recrossing the entrance to the chapel, Kevin kept genuflecting to the Presence!

I saw men tip their hats when crossing in front of a church when I was a child, but to drop to one knee when crossing in front of a church, repeatedly? Never. But Christ was present. That was enough for Kevin.

All the powers of a fine mind turned to "religion" and religious things, and then this fool of a man for Christ—it seemed like an accusation.

Meeting Kevin disquieted me that evening.

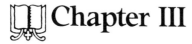 # Chapter III

The North Bank of the River Liffey: Queen Street

After living in Stormanstown for only a few years, Catherine's father, who was over fifty when he married his young wife, died. To be near relatives, his widow moved into apartments she owned on Queen Street in Dublin.

So, after a few days of reflection and writing, I went looking for Queen Street. With my backpack filled with sketching materials and a raincoat, I boarded the bus, got off at Daniel O'Connell's statue and started walking along the north bank of the river.

It seemed that every man and woman in Ireland was on the streets that morning, along with bicycles and big diesel trucks headed south. There was even a convoy of jeeps and weapon-carriers filled with soldiers dressed in green, their machine guns in their laps. Through it all I waded, past run-down stores, abandoned tenements, small fruit, candy and newspaper stores, always away from the crowd, along Mary Street, Little Mary Street, Abbey Street.

This whole area bordering the north bank of the River Liffey had once been a Cistercian abbey called St. Mary's, with spacious lands, churches, a monastery and farms. Now the only reminders of the abbey were the names of the streets.

Thirty minutes later I came to Queen Street. It was still early in the morning and I felt refreshed by the walk in the brisk autumn air. Positioning myself between a fence and a telephone pole, I faced the river. Looking across the river, I sketched the magnificent twelfth century cathedral, Christ Church, a familiar landmark for Dubliners for a thousand years. Beside it were the two buildings the McAuley family probably owned. They were built in 1770, sixteen years before Catherine's birth. Here was her neighborhood.

Mrs. McAuley didn't outlive her husband by much, dying a few years later, when Catherine was twelve. The apartments on Queen Street were then sold,

The Queen Street apartments

and Catherine's portion of the money from the sale was invested by her relatives in a new kind of school that was just getting started called the Apothecaries Hall. A school for the training of doctors, pharmacists and midwives, it was located only a few blocks away, on Mary Street. At the age of twelve, Catherine became a stockholder in a profession that was to have a lasting influence on her.

After the death of her mother, Catherine, her brother and her sister were passed from one relative to another—and, as a result, from one faith to another, for some of their relatives were non-Catholic. The deaths in her family and the moving about created a good deal of instability in Catherine's life.

Since many of the people she lived with for the next fifteen years, as well as the Apothecaries Hall itself, were located on Mary Street, I decided to head there. It seemed to me to hold a clue to one of the significant influences in her life. Today, Catherine's followers care for the sick in hospitals throughout the world. Did her interest in the poor and the sick, I wondered, start with an investment in the Apothecaries Hall?

After a day of sketching and exploring Dublin, I walked the crowded streets, at dusk, looking for a place to eat. I bought a paper from Susie, a short, heavy woman with a face pushed out of shape by a lifetime of laughing, living and telling good stories. She sat at the narrow entrance to a basement restaurant. On her recommendation I went inside and bought a plateful of sausages and eggs.

Reflecting over tea, I came to the conclusion that, in Dublin, there was some kind of strange understanding between pedestrians and car drivers regarding the traffic lights. At a certain moment, a wave of people simply moved across the street, whatever the color of the lights at the intersection. The cars and buses all stopped. At other times, the people on foot sensed that this was not the time to move. They stood and waited. The cars and buses then had their turn.

Later in the evening, I sat in my small room at All Hallows College, an unshaded lightbulb shining on green, faded walls, my feet propped up on a chair, and continued my reflections. Dublin was beginning to have meaning for me. And Catherine's past was coming more and more to life.

The following morning I went back into Dublin, to the street where Catherine spent a fourth of her life—her formative years. I walked to the intersection of Mary and Liffey Streets and stopped, looking at what was going on around me: Mary Street! Bulging at the seams with activity and people, especially on weekends. Today was Saturday, and it was impossible to walk in a straight line. I had to wade through the street—it was as if I were stalled on a freeway of wall-to-wall people.

The Moore Street open-air market, which emptied out onto Mary Street, was even more densely packed with people of every description: ladies wheeling their latest offspring, smart young couples, college people dressed in a way that would match any cosmopolitan city in the world. An old blind man tapped his way along the street with a broken cane, eyes vacant, clothes stained with food and drink dripped on the way to his mouth. There were people with humped backs and open cancers eating away at their faces. There were strong men, lovely women, cripples, beggars and always the old.

The world of the medieval surrealist Hieronymus Bosch was not so distant after all, but right here on a Dublin street, alongside the posh, smart women in expensive furs and leather boots, and well-dressed businessmen.

This was life on Mary and Liffey Streets, where disease, poverty and wealth are all accepted facts. So, too, is death. Where a multitude of stone virgins and statues of the Sacred Heart look down on the Dubliners, accepted by them as a true symbol of what life is *also* about: that God loves them.

I felt strongly attracted to this intersection and had the sense that this was the Dublin Catherine knew as a teenager living on this street. How right I was I didn't discover until later. Signs, buildings, pubs and people! The whole human race was gathered together at this intersection. Was it so different in Catherine's time? In 1880, when she was fourteen years old and living close by, there was an average of eighteen people living in each house on Mary Street. And the houses were butted up

23

Christ Church

against each other, supporting each other in fact: a depressing picture considering that the art of medicine was still at the barbershop stage. Extreme poverty was common. The stark differences between the rich and the poor were all around her, like the crowds on Mary Street.

I simply yielded to the impact of people, buildings and all the activity taking place, sketching it all. It was marvelous. Alive. And right into the midst of all this traffic an older gentleman came down the street, pushing a cart for rubbish, dressed in a suit and tie. Delayed by his slow progress and dedication to duty, people, trucks and cars backed up behind him. But they waited. And the whole thing worked itself out. When he had finished what he had come there for, the congestion cleared.

I was impressed with the woodwork of the pub on the corner of Mary and Liffey Streets, The Elbow Inn, so in my sketch I included as much of it as I could, and a little of the building next to it. What I didn't know until later in the afternoon was that Catherine had lived in this building, 31 Mary Street, next to where the pub now stands.

One of the relatives Catherine lived with after her mother's death was a man named Dr. Armstrong, of Mary Street. Through him, Catherine met one of his relatives, a chemist named Mr. William Callaghan who taught at the Apothecaries Hall. That meeting resulted in a lifelong friendship with Mr. Callaghan since he invited Catherine to come live with him and his wife. Both were Protestant. Catherine accepted.

After I finished the sketch of the crowded intersection, I packed and started walking west toward Queen Street. From somewhere above me, on the opposite side of the street, I heard a dog barking. The crowd had thinned so I stopped, trying to figure out why the sound was coming from above. On the top story of the building next to The Elbow Inn a dog sat in an open window. Behind him was a young lady and, since I needed directions, I shouted up: ''Could you tell me where 47 Mary Street is?'' The address was one that I thought was correct for the Apothecaries Hall, but which I wasn't able to locate.

In a voice used to dealing with strangers—and common in large cities—she shouted down: "Yeah. Down the block there." She gestured vaguely and I looked in that direction.

"Thanks," I shouted back, unsure of what I had learned by asking. Then my eyes moved down the face of the building. Printed in large letters on a sign that extended over the sidewalk were the words "31 Mary Street." But what really caught my attention was a gigantic barber pole attached to the building that projected horizontally over the sidewalk. It looked ancient, as though it had been there a good hundred and fifty years.

The barber pole, even as late as the nineteenth century, was the symbol for the barber-surgeon: red for blood and white for bandage.

Number 31, the building next to the pub! It dawned on me that Catherine had lived here with a chemist and his wife, right across the street from the Apothecaries Hall. How close everything seemed to be in her life. I unpacked my gear and started another sketch.

An hour later I took a last look at the building and the barber pole—a relic, and a reminder, of what went on in this building over a century ago, for often a professional person had his place of business on the bottom floor while he and his family lived above the "shop."

On the way back to All Hallows College, I felt satisfied that I had discovered something concrete about Catherine's surroundings, and the person she was quite close to, Mr. Callaghan. I remembered having seen a painting of him in her room at Baggot Street, but knowing little about his background I had not paid too much attention to it. Now I would have to revisit Baggot Street House to take a good look at the man with whom Catherine lived and from whom she inherited the fortune she needed to do the work God called her to do.

Supper at All Hallows, a seminary for training missionary priests, was quite an experience, with a certain monastic flavor to it. The dining room was immense and poorly lighted. It had an extremely high ceiling. The priests and visitors sat on one side of the room, along the wall. The seminarians sat at right angles to the priests' tables. Everyone talked until the bell was

Mary and Liffey Streets

rung, when there was a sudden up-surge of bodies, and over a hundred men stood up and shoved their chairs back under the tables. In perfect silence they said grace, followed by a procession of sorts down the windy, Gothic corridor to a chapel hardly big enough to hold everyone, where a visit was made and a prayer for vocations recited. After the visit, pandemonium: everyone started talking at once.

Later that night I reworked the sketches, wrote in my diary and walked down the narrow hallway, lighted by a solitary bulb. I went down four flights of stairs and into the kitchen, where two young boys worked when they were not waiting on tables. After work they usually watched television, an American and British variety filled with violence, sex and crime. This particular night they talked to each other in such a rapid-fire brogue that I couldn't understand them at first, but I strongly suspected their remarks were off-color.

We sat around a thick, wooden table used for carving, eating and holding containers of food. Along the wall were huge pots and pans; below them, heavy iron sinks. Tucked away in a corner was the television set.

There was a soft knock on the door that led out into the courtyard in front of the Gothic chapel nearby. The boys looked at each other, went to the door and started talking with someone. Then they returned, got some coffee and food and brought it out to Kevin, who stood outside begging a meal. This was a regular ritual that no one was supposed to know about—no one in authority, that is, especially the matron of the house. But everyone knew about it and looked the other way.

When the boys learned that I was an artist their eyes lit up. They asked me to copy something they had pinned on the wall of their room. I expected a movie actress or a rock star, but instead they brought down holy cards that were given to them by a priest in their hometown, pictures of Saint Martin de Porres with a protective arm around a few young boys. These cards were perhaps the only comfort these two had so far from home. So perhaps my ear had misled me. These boys, who I thought were telling off-color jokes, had, like Kevin, found strength in their religion.

30

The following morning, on my way to the house that Catherine built, I tried riding on the top deck of the double-decker bus. We careened against curb stops, picking up and disgorging passengers as we moved steadily down into the "Black Hole," as some Dubliners refer to their city.

Once more I met Sister Finian, the superior, and shared some tea with her. Mr. Callaghan's picture in the room where Catherine had died meant more to me now that I had seen the place where he had lived and practiced as a chemist. "How appropriate," I thought, "in this ecumenical age, that the only other picture in this Catholic room is that of a Protestant man."

Mr. Callaghan and his wife were a wealthy couple. They invited Catherine into their home and eventually bequeathed to her their home, fortune and land—at a time when the relationships between Protestants and Catholics were often strained. Why did they do it? The answer is spelled out in Mr. Callaghan's will, where he gives all "to my kind and affectionate friend, Miss Catherine McAuley, who resides with me, for her many kindnesses and atten-

tions." He changed his will at the last moment, in an attached codicil, making her the sole "legatee of all my estates and effects." Catherine was that much of a friend to him and his wife that Mr. Callaghan even wanted her to take his name as her own.

I looked at the picture carefully. What an interesting face the man had. He had obviously posed for the painting, and the artist had used soft pastels in depicting his subject. I made a sketch from it. Good as the painting was, I discovered that Mr. Callaghan's face was better suited to my black and white version than the colors of the painting. His features gained strength; his face looked patrician.

As I drew, I sat on a piece of furniture that once belonged to him. I thought, "I know he was a chemist and governor of the Apothecaries Hall on Mary Street—but where on Mary Street?" Supposedly it was near Catherine's home at number 31, but I had seen no sign of it the day before.

I asked Sister Finian, but she had no idea. Nor did the other sisters. Apparently there were no pictures or records. But I did get a suggestion: "Why not go

31

31 Mary Street

to the library and look up the Builder's Book, a historical record of what buildings were built and when?"

I left the sisters and walked over to the nearby National Library, but all I could find was a brief notice that in 1900 there had been a "fire in the rere of the Apothecaries Hall on Mary Street." No address, though at least I was now sure that the hall had stood on Mary Street.

When someone pointed out to me that there was an Apothecaries Hall in operation very close to where I was, in south Dublin, finding the original hall became a mystery to be solved. It had been on Mary Street. Now it was on the south side of Dublin, not far from the Mercy Sisters. From the library I went to the address of the present hall, close to the administrative and military core of the Republic of Ireland.

The whole area bristled with tight security and government business. Black, spike-tipped fences kept out the visitor who couldn't flash a special pass. I walked past the formidable buildings, down a row of Georgian houses, through a double door and up a long flight of stairs that curved into a large room, filled with young men seeking credentials in first aid.

They were all nervously awaiting the results of their examinations. Beyond the smoke, hanging on the wall, was a list of all the governors of the Apothecaries Hall from its beginnings in 1791. Finally, a link with the original hall! And among the names of the former governors were William Callaghan and Catherine's uncle, Dr. William Armstrong. Strangely enough, when I asked, no one knew anything about the original hall.

A portly doctor, out of breath and in a hurry, took an interest in my search and led me into a small back room. He opened a locker set against the wall—surprise: out of it came the original mace, symbolizing the royal charter granted to the Apothecaries Hall back in 1790. It was old, dusty and worn with use. The next treasures to come out of the locker were a cloak and tricorn hat worn by the mace-bearer when certificates of completion were granted to graduates. He told me that the present hall still had its original charter.

On my way out of the building I met the son of the doctor in charge of the hall and we struck up a conversation. I told him I was confused about the location of the original hall. His reaction was quick: "Why don't you go to the National Library and look it up?"

"I tried that," I said, "and didn't have much luck. I looked through past newspapers—"

"No, I'm not talking about that. Why don't you get *Thom's Street Index* for 1790 and find out what businesses and professions were located on Mary Street at that time?"

I didn't know there was such a book. "Look," he said, "let's go to the library together, and I'll show you where the books are."

The two of us walked back to the library, up the marble stairs and into the room I had visited before. My new-found friend spoke a few quiet words with the librarian, and doors opened into the world of the reserved books. As I passed into the inner sanctum, I tried looking Irish, but the librarian ignored me with a look of barely concealed disdain. But oh, the books were real treasures. And there on the top shelf was a whole row of faded, green volumes, titled *Thom's Street Index*, which dated back to 1790 and listed all the professional people living on the main streets of Dublin, as well as their places of business. In the back of each book was a finely etched map of the Dublin area for that year. From those books I got the exact address of the Apothecaries Hall: 40 Mary Street. I also got the addresses of Catherine's relatives and friends who were connected with medicine, among whom, of course, was Mr. Callaghan, who lived at 31 Mary Street and above the hall before he moved out into the country.

That night I again ate with the assembled community of All Hallows College, feeling very conspicuous in that vast, poorly lighted dining room, filled with oversized pictures of the college's famous alumni: bishops, deans and teachers. They all seemed to stare down at me from the walls—and I still hadn't completely tuned my ear to the Irish accent.

That evening I resolved to go down to the Mary Street area and sketch the Apothecaries Hall over which Catherine had lived.

William Callaghan

 # Chapter IV

The Apothecaries Hall

I got a rare ride into Dublin the next afternoon in an automobile. After being left off on O'Connell Street, I passed the Liberator's statue and walked to Mary Street, where cars were not allowed. Once more I saw the smartly dressed women in furs, the street urchins and the beggars singing for a few pence. The louder the beggars sang, it seemed, the more money was dropped into the waiting cardboard boxes. Their voices were strident, high-pitched and wailing.

From my right the smell of fresh vegetables and garbage came to me from the open-air market on Moore Street, along with the cries of hawkers and the singing of beggars. I felt as if I were in the middle of a circus. I was on my way to 40 Mary Street.

But what a surprise when I got there and discovered the Apothecaries Hall! I had passed this building many times, yet hadn't really seen it. I could now see why. I had looked only at the bottom story where a nightclub and television store occupied what used to be the grand entrance to the hall.

So this was the well-known nineteenth century Apothecaries Hall, the training school for doctors, midwives and pharmacists. It had taken me quite a while to find this building, so it was satisfying to step into the abandoned entrance and sketch it. By the time I finished, the sun was beginning to go down and the sidewalk traffic was thinning. I tried the door of the nightclub, which was abandoned, but it was padlocked. I had hoped to go upstairs and look at the meeting rooms over which Catherine had lived. From below, I could see that the upper stories of the building were vacant, and had been for some time, perhaps since the mysterious fire in 1900, when the whole operation had to be moved south of the river.

From a booklet given me by a member of the present hall, I read that the hall was started by a Dr. Charles Lucas,

Certificate of graduation from the Hall

APOTHECARIES' HALL OF DUBLIN
IRELAND

To all to whom these Presents shall come Greeting
Know ye that We the Governor Deputy Governor & Court
OF THE APOTHECARIES HALL OF DUBLIN

have caused _____ to be
publicly and solemnly Examined in the Principles and Practice of
MEDICINE, SURGERY, MIDWIFERY AND PHARMACY.
The Examiners having Certified to us that _____ possesses a competent knowledge
of these subjects we therefore hereby admit _____ a Licenciate, of the Apothecaries
Hall of Dublin and authorise _____ to practise the said Arts and Sciences accordingly
Given under our hands and seal at Dublin
this _____ day of _____ 19 ____

_____ Governor

_____ Deputy Governor

Court

N°. _____ Enrolled by _____ Registrar & Secretary

an Irish patriot who "fell foul of the Castle authorities and fled to England, and after to France." Before he "fell foul," he thought up the idea of a guild of apothecaries that would supply "competent medical advice and curative drugs at a nominal fee in remote country districts." Since the sixteenth-century suppression of the monasteries, to which infirmaries and hospitals were often attached, the poor, when sick, were "constrained to go either to a gaol, lunatic asylum, or fever hospital in quest for medical aid." Not too many options. And there were plenty of quacks to take what little money they did have. Dr. Lucas applied for and received a charter for a guild of fraternity of apothecaries, in which the art and "mystery" of medicine would be taught and practiced. The royal charter needed to do such a thing was received in 1742.

The original fraternity was called the Guild of Saint Luke, since Luke, the writer of the third gospel, has traditionally been associated with doctors.

The guild was a successful attempt at eliminating some of the crackpots in the field of pharmacy and medicine. A guild of interested pharmacists and doctors was not enough, however. A sorely needed place of training was applied for in 1790, and, as a result, the Irish Apothecaries Act was passed in that year, and a hall built at 40 Mary Street.

The original members of the Apothecary Guild had to swear an oath against Transubstantiation, the explanation the Catholic Church uses to describe the real presence of Jesus Christ in the Eucharist. From its beginning, St. Luke's Guild had a distinctly Protestant leaning.

That evening I decided it was time for me to get out of Dublin for a while—too many crowds, too many people I would never get to know, too much activity. I needed a change of scenery: from the city into the country, from the crowded streets into the open fields, from tenements to the grand homes outside Dublin. Catherine had moved into one of these mansions in 1809 with Mr. and Mrs. Callaghan when she was twenty-three years old. That mansion was now a Mercy convent called Coolock House.

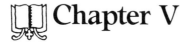 # Chapter V

A Mansion in the Country: Coolock House

On a World War I vintage telephone, I called one of the Sisters of Mercy at Coolock House and asked for instructions on how to get there. "Out Malahide Road," she said, "and get off at the Coolock district."

Once more I packed my sketching materials, raincoat, hat and a few books and started walking, but this time away from the city, up and out into the modest but lovely hills of northeast Dublin.

I had been told to walk to Malahide, about three miles from where I was staying. From there I would take a bus north. While waiting for the bus, I did a sketch of the intersection since the buildings seemed quite old. It was an overcast day, with the oily smell of diesel fuel clinging to everything; there

was almost no wind. It began to drizzle and in the light, fine mist, I waited along with the others for the Coolock bus to come. The bus was filled with schoolchildren, and I was struck with how different they seemed from the children playing around the flats where Catherine was born—perhaps because these children were returning to homes, not slabs of concrete stacked together like tombs.

I got off at the Coolock exit and walked a few blocks until I came to two stone pillars that once marked the edge of the estate. What a lovely piece of ground it was. A painting of it at Coolock, done in the nineteenth century, shows the expansive fields, the trees, gently rolling hills and horses, with the mansion as the centerpiece.

This was Catherine's home from 1809 to 1822, when Mr. Callaghan died and left her his entire estate. Here Catherine led the life of a lady—but the will of Mr. Callaghan makes it clear that this was not all she was doing, for it singles out her kindness and attention to him and his wife, which must have been present all along or it would not have shown up in the will.

Pot's Hall

What a change had taken place from the time Catherine first came here. A primary and secondary school of two thousand girls now occupied the space where horses galloped. Catherine's investment in time, love and money had paid off in an unexpected way, for though she sold this property to get money to help the poor, by a fine twist of fate the Sisters of Mercy recently had the chance to buy it back.

I went up the stairs to the mansion, noticing the iron grill-work and the circular drive. It was a fine, well-built home, impressive by any standards. After I knocked, one of the sisters came to the door and I identified myself. A welcome awaited me.

The first thing I noticed inside the door to Coolock House was the space: a wide receiving room flanked by dining rooms and parlors. At the end of the vestibule was a winding staircase that led to the second floor and the bedroom area, where the sisters lived. With its gracefulness, the staircase was quite a contrast to the world I had been working in for weeks, so when I finished tea, I sat just inside the entrance door and did a drawing of it, trying to imagine the many people from Dublin who were just as impressed as I was when they walked through the front door a hundred and fifty years ago. Sisters whom I had not met passed by me, going and coming to school. They acted as if it were the most normal thing in the world for a stranger to sit in the entranceway and sketch the staircase.

Next I was shown all over the house: the room Catherine lived in and the room next to hers where Mrs. Callaghan lived and in which, when dying, she was nursed by Catherine.

While living at Coolock House, Catherine grew in her own faith, but only after what seems to have been a crisis. She had doubts, probably brought on by the different religions she was subjected to, and the often hostile religious discussions that took place among the better educated. Another reason may have been the kindness and the sophistication of the family with whom she was living. They were good people. She loved them. And they were Protestant. Still, she had been born a Catholic, though she spent a good deal of her time living with non-Catholics.

The worm of doubt and confusion

gnawed away within her conscience, bursting out of its hiding place when she moved into the country. What was the right thing for *her* to do, the right way for *her* to live? That had to be resolved. And now she had the time and the urgency to resolve it. Fortunately, she was directed to a man who would have a significant impression on her life, both directly, through his teachings, and indirectly, through his other students. The man's name was Thomas Beytagh, a Jesuit priest.

Thomas Beytagh was an old man when Catherine met him, and he had lived through the worst of the penal days, when the laws against Catholics were strictly enforced. He had also lived through the suppression, by the Catholic Church, of the company of men to whom he belonged, the Society of Jesus. After the suppression of the Jesuits, Thomas Beytagh became an underground priest in the service of the poor, one who surreptitiously taught the young the faith that was outlawed, a capital offense in eighteenth-century Ireland.

The schools that Beytagh started were concealed in basements, attics and back rooms on streets whose names were a description of what went on in those streets: Skinner's Row, where the tanners worked; Cook's Street; Fishamble Street—exotic names matched only by the names of nearby pubs like the Black Dog Inn, the Ship's Tavern, the Sign of the Harp, and the Old Robin Hood. Father Beytagh had schools on all these streets where the faith was secretly taught to young boys. In his classrooms sat the future leaders of the Church in Ireland, some of whom became Catherine's close friends.

It was to this great and good man—described by a contemporary as an excellent example of the scholar of penal days—that Catherine came with her doubts. And little by little, they were resolved. Her own faith came more clearly into focus.

During this time she also became more concerned with the poor and the uneducated, especially with young women. Perhaps this concern was due, in part, to her talks with Father Beytagh. She could see, after all, what he had done for the boys in the poor schools. She also saw, while she was living in the city and at Coolock, the

Malahide Road

pressing need to do something for the girls. She wanted to save them from the streets, from ignorance. She wanted to give them a trade and communicate to them the faith she was growing in. As she grew older, this idea appeared with more urgency. How rapidly, she wrote, the days, weeks and months were passing. Another month ended, when it seemed as if only a few days had gone by.

My own day was going by fast. There were a few more drawings I wanted to do, so when I finished my tour of the mansion, I went outside the house, beyond the circular driveway, and sat beneath a centuries-old oak. There I started a sketch of the house, reflecting that many fine carriages from Dublin had come into this driveway; and many fine ladies escorted by well-dressed gentlemen had walked up the stairs to be greeted by the young lady, Catherine. She was, after all, essential to the entertainment, since many of the people who visited Coolock were her relatives. She enjoyed a party. Even after she inherited a fortune and knew what she was going to do with it, she entertained. In the words of a contemporary Englishman, she was no dry-as-dust do-gooder.

While sketching, I could hear dogs barking in the distance and the sounds of children playing. Then two small girls came through the gates of the estate and into the driveway. They climbed the stairs and rang the doorbell. They waited, looking at each other and at the door. After a bit, it opened and a Sister of Mercy bent down to talk to them.

There are stories from Catherine's earliest biographies that from this time on she began to teach the children who lived nearby simple truths about God and His love for men and women. And she was also interested in relieving the poverty she saw, so she brought out food from the house for them. I was happy to see that the tradition continued.

When I finished the drawing of the mansion, I left the property, crossed the crowded Malahide Road and walked down a side street to the Chapel of St. Brendan, named after the legendary sea traveler. This was Catherine's parish church while living at Coolock House, easily within walking distance.

What a massive structure! Thick and sturdy, built like a fort with a slate roof, it originally might have been no more than a barn with a thatched roof:

In the forty-odd years between the union and the famine all over Ireland ''newly built slated chapels'' replaced the low thatched barns or even ''mass rocks'' and ''mass gardens'' of the penal area.

The lack of a steeple—forbidden by law to Catholic places of worship—designated it as a chapel, and chapels were forbidden on main streets. So St. Brendan's is tucked away at back of the main road.

In the middle of doing a drawing, two young girls came up to me to watch. The older one, a thin, pretty red-headed girl with blue eyes, looked at the picture and said, ''Oh! Isn't it lovely! Are you an artist?''

I said, ''Yes, I am.'' Then I explained that I was doing a book on Catherine.

''Oh. Catherine McAuley! I go to her school.''

I asked her what her name was, and her answer came right out of antiquity: Emer. She was so open, interested and articulate that I offered her the sketch I was working on. Her response was immediate: her eyes lit up. She took the sketch, thought for a moment and handed it back to me, asking me to autograph it. After I gave it back to her, she looked at it fondly, then—ever so politely—folded it right down the middle and put it into her satchel.

After I left Emer and her friend, I walked down the street, turned and did another sketch of St. Brendan's. On the bus back to All Hallow's College, I thought of Catherine and of the money she inherited, 25,000 pounds! A friend of Mr. Callaghan's expressed some surprise and doubt about leaving her so much. Mr. Callaghan's response was: ''Don't worry, she will know what to do with it.'' He knew from living with her that she would use it for the poor. By willing his fortune to her, he knew he was investing in her and in the work of Jesus Christ. He was far from being opposed to her interest in religion and the poor. He himself made provisions for the poor of St. Brendan's parish in his will, when he gave ''to the poor of the parish of Coolock, the sum of thirty

Coolock House

pounds to be distributed as my executors hereafter named may think proper.''

While living at Coolock, Catherine strengthened her relationships with those who were interested in the same goals she was: men and women concerned with teaching the faith and removing the ignorance, injustice and poverty so prevalent in nineteenth-century Ireland. One such friend was James Nugent, the pastor of St. Brendan's from 1821 to 1823. Some of his enthusiasm he communicated to Catherine. Together they traveled into Dublin to teach and help in the schools for the poor that had sprung up on Middle Abbey Street, near where she had been living before moving to Coolock.

Now I rode in that direction, away from the seventeen Sisters of Mercy who lived in Catherine's mansion, though not in her room, which was kept open for the many people who visited there and for other, deeper reasons.

When I arrived home it was late. I was cold. I climbed the four flights to my room, sat in the chair and looked hopefully at the heater, an S-curved pipe about nine inches in diameter that snaked its way into my room, did a turn and went back out. The scheduled date for turning it on was October 1, and even though this was only September 15, it was freezing! The only way I could get warm was to fill the water basin with hot water from the tap and plunge my arms into it up to my elbows.

That evening I went to bed with the intention of finding out the poor schools that Catherine and Father Nugent taught in. The only clue I had was that they were near the Apothecaries Hall and on Middle Abbey Street.

Before I slept, I wrote into my diary a prayer of dependence and hope, a prayer thanking God that he had called me here, to this place and time, to do this work:

Here
I am,
Lord,
At this moment.
You called.
Thank you.
I hope my life
Brings honor
To your name.

What could I long for
That you haven't made
　possible?
Yet even this is not enough—
　The work of art, after all,
　Leads back
　To the artist!
What I really want
Is you.
That is the hope
Behind all my activity;
And that is what you
　created me for.
Do with me then,
What you will.

That night I had a disturbing dream that I was seated in a comfortable, over-stuffed chair, doing a sketch, eating and listening to a radio. I was listening with only half an ear to the beat of Jamaican music, simply background, but then I began to focus on the meaning of the words. Here they are, as far as I can remember them, sung in a voice filled with sorrow and humility:

　Oh my God!
　Oh my God!
　What world is this
　That man must live in trial?

Oh my God!
Oh my God!
Make the rich man
Love the poor man,
And the world will be
the best it can...
Oh my God!
Oh my God!

I stopped sketching and listened attentively to the words, for I felt disturbed by them. Someone cooked my meals. People called me "father." I had received many talents and the leisure to develop them. I was the rich in the song, and the Jamaicans, the Haitians, the El Salvadorans—the poor beggars on the streets of Dublin and all over the world, were singing in my ear!

　Oh my God!
　Oh my God!
　Make the rich man
　Love the poor man,
　And the world will be
　The best it can...

I woke with a feeling of uneasiness, even fear, feelings similar to those I had when I met Kevin. In the half-dark room I lay awake for a long time and wished for dawn.

The winding staircase, Coolock House

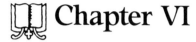 # Chapter VI

Back on the Streets

The name *Dublin* comes from the Irish *Duibhlinn*, which means "black pool." I reflected on the name as I went into the city the next morning. According to historians, the name derived from a deep pool at the back of a castle situated at the heart of the city in pre-Viking times. Dublin was a city with a long history, and I was looking for some of that history now as I returned to the city.

While looking for the site of the poor schools I discovered that there were no actual sites because the poor schools happened wherever they could. There is no sign left of them. But while searching I came upon a huge brick structure that occupied half a city block. Seeing no entrance, I circled it and came to the back of Jervis Street Hospital, only a block away from the Apothecaries Hall.

I was fascinated by the overhanging balconies and the building's nineteenth-century look, so I went into the hospital, looking for the main desk. There was none—I simply found myself in a corridor. I walked around for a while, trying to discover how to contact a secretary, doctor or nurse. I wanted to discover how long the hospital had been there. I wanted to know something of its past. Finally I was directed to an opening in the corridor. Four or five people were standing along a dingy wall, obviously in pain of some kind or another. To my untrained eye they looked like they needed immediate help.

A nurse passed me, followed by someone dressed in green. The patients along the wall groaned. No one attended them. They waited. I looked at the floor of the corridor, littered with pieces of crumpled paper, what I thought looked like garbage. When I visited the restroom I noticed that the lock had been torn loose, along with the wood around it. There was water, or urine, an inch deep on the floor. The

Father Beytagh, the Underground Priest

toilet didn't work. I began to feel dirty, on the verge of catching a disease were I to remain much longer in that hospital. Meanwhile, the patients stood without being helped, without so much as a chair to sit on.

I was about to leave when I noticed a man in green. Unlike the other hospital attendants he wasn't moving anywhere, so I asked him for the name of the hospital, and something about its history. Did he have a booklet that would give me some information? I got an immediate response. He did not know that I was a priest, but he did know I was an American. With a number of unattended patients humbly waiting in pain, the man in green asked me to wait; then he got two nurses and the three of them explained the history of the hospital, telling me where I could find more. All this took considerable time, and I felt like a member of the privileged class. The people standing against the wall were forgotten while I chatted with the attendant and nurses.

The Jervis Street Hospital was, in its outside corridors, the dirtiest hospital I had ever been in. It was quite different in the inner wards, but I still found it hard to believe that the Sisters of Mercy were in charge. I wondered what Catherine McAuley would do and say were she waiting in line, backed up against a wall, amidst such dirt.

The hospital was only a block or two from where Catherine grew up and only down the street from the Apothecaries Hall. It seemed to me that no matter which way one turned a hundred and fifty years ago, he ran into medicine.

I left the hospital and went back onto the streets, but I didn't find any poor schools. I suppose I expected some kind of plaque detailing where the poor schools had been, but Dublin is far too complex and far too old a city for that.

It was easy to locate Coolock House and Baggot Street House since they were still standing, marked. But it was impossible to locate the precise place where Catherine taught the poor in the poor schools on Middle Abbey Street—impossible because of the density of historical events in the city that preceded and accompanied Catherine's life. The difference between the country, where there is plenty of space, and the heart of Dublin, where layer upon layer of history has to be peeled back, is tremendous. Names of streets have changed, as well as the streets themselves. Churches and chapels have been torn down or their names have been changed—even their allegiance. It is not a simple matter of stumbling upon a bronzed plaque with some such inscription: "Here, Catherine McAuley, founder of the Sisters of Mercy, taught the poor." The "here" is likely to be a pub, and before that a tenement or a disguised, back-street chapel—and even before that, the scene of a battle—and long before that, stretching back into history, a Viking stronghold or a sacred pool. Dublin is, indeed, so densely packed with history that a historian would not know how to squeeze all that has happened in one location onto one brass plaque. Channels and networks of historical events criss-cross each other just below the surface of the asphalt roads, breaking upward and outward in impressive monuments like Christ Church and Dublin Castle. They, it seems, have resisted time.

Once I realized that there were no poor schools to be found, I walked over to the Mary and Liffey Street area, just to observe. At least I was within a block or two from where the poor schools *used* to be. Once again, I took out my sketch pad and surrendered to the impact of people and movement. Once again, I was taken by a scene filled with human energy, poverty and riches—but I wasn't so taken that I didn't hear the eerie cry of the small street beggars, children, who sit on the cement pavement entertaining with their plaintive songs and wail their way into the human heart and pocketbook. Some of these children were lynx-eyed, sharp and aware of everything going on in the streets. Others seemed listless and dejected. I passed one girl who had half of her scalp missing; folded scar tissue covered the right side of her head. Like the other children, she had her cardboard box, only she wasn't holding it out toward passers-by. It rested in her lap. Medicine could have helped her, I thought, could have removed the disfigurement. I bent over to ask her what had happened to scar her so badly. She looked up and said, "I was burned by scalding water when I was a baby."

I thought: My God! You're not much

63

St. Brendan's Chapel, Coolock

more than a baby now! Out loud I said, "What would you do if I gave you some money?"

"Buy some food," she answered. I emptied my purse into the small cardboard box.

She was a stray, a vagabond, a beggar, a child of the streets, begging and scavenging for a living, the kind that preyed on Catherine's mind. During the two important years following Mr. Callaghan's death, she began to formulate a plan for the distribution of her wealth. She wanted to build a house, a house for the poor, like the small beggar girl I met on the street, a home for young girls who couldn't make it on their own, a place where they could be taught and reinforced in their faith, find shelter and learn some skills to survive.

I had given all I had in my change purse to the scarred beggar girl, but Catherine had given all she had—a considerable amount. I returned home that evening, thoughtful. The day's events had made a deep impression on me.

# Chapter VII

A Home for the Poor: Crisis and Decision

In 1824 Catherine purchased a piece of property on the south side of the city, home of the middle class, and laid the cornerstone for what was to become the first of many such houses all over the world, a House of Mercy. Her letters reveal why she picked the south side for the house. Identifying the people who contributed in large part to the building up of the church in the nineteenth century, she observed:

The rich do comparatively little for religion. And the poor cannot afford to do much. The middle class is the most influential class. It gives the best priests and religious to the church. It gives employment to the poor. It builds our chapels, it supports our charitable institutions.

She had few illusions about the value and use of money:

You will excuse me, I am sure...for you know although I should be simple as a dove, I must also be prudent as a Serpent; and since there is very little good can be accomplished or evil avoided without the aid of money, we must look after it in small as well as in great matters.

So with a realistic attitude about what she could do with what she had been given, she purchased land and hired a builder. The house was built in an open field, bordered in front by a street. It took four years to build, and adopted the name of the street: Baggot Street House.

Building a three-story house on the south side of Dublin certainly didn't take place without provoking jealousy and opposition, especially among Catherine's relatives and, later, the clergy. She was, after all, an unmarried, thirty-six year-old woman who had inherited a fortune and wanted to spend it all on a house for the poor. Her brother, James, a doctor, implied that she was unbalanced and spoke of her plan to build the home as a "stupid waste of money, supporting the most worthless people in the city."

Jervis Street Hospital

What provoked that remark? James was eager to see her use the money she had inherited to attain a high position in society. According to one of the earliest lives of Catherine, a major of an estate called Bellevue House had repeatedly proposed to her without luck. The major went to James to see if he would intercede for him. James attempted to persuade Catherine by criticizing her for foolishly spending her money on the Baggot House scheme and refusing at the same time the opportunity of becoming the wife of a major. The dialogue went something like this:

James: You're foolish, Catherine, for spending your money and time on a home for the poor; and for refusing an offer to become the mistress of Bellevue House!

Catherine: I quitted a nicer house than that, James.

James: Yes. You would rather build this stupid looking concern, and support the most worthless people in this city. What has become of your good sense? Those who love you are aggrieved and ashamed of you; those who don't know you are laughing at you. Give up these nonsensical whims, and live as a lady does. A warm welcome awaits you at Bellevue.

Catherine: Awaits me, or my fortune?

But it had been obvious as early as 1822 that Catherine was up to something. As the new mistress of the Coolock estate, she had organized a regular method for distributing food to the poor. She was teaching in the poor schools with Father Nugent, and she had adopted some stray beggar girls who were living with her. She had also made a trip to France to study the latest educational methods, said to be the best in Europe. So the cornerstone for the three-story house for the poor on the south side of Dublin should not have been such a surprise.

Catherine's efforts, however, were not without the support and very determined direction of the clergy—a direction that quickly resulted in another crisis in her life. Because of the Church's involvement, she soon found that she would have either to surrender the completed house to the diocese or enter a religious order.

The forces that provoked the crisis

70

were at work even before the house was built. She and two priest-consultants came up with a plan for a large, spacious, rather simple building, with four large rooms to be used as schools for the poor, dormitories for distressed women, a chapel and smaller rooms where the women helping Catherine could stay overnight. But what emerged was a large house filled with corridors, cells, dividing grates and high monastic windows. Her rather simple plans for the house had been changed, and were not discovered until the house was built.

Someone other than Catherine had changed the plans, someone who had very definite ideas about what this house was going to be used for: a convent. When Catherine mentioned that the house was beginning to look very much like a convent in appearance, one of her advisors, a Reverend Mr. Armstrong, is reported to have said, "We did not anticipate this, but God has his own designs in it."

Baggot Street House rose slowly over the next four years, and during that time Catherine's energies were focused on what could be accomplished once it was opened. She visited parents whose children needed, but couldn't afford, schooling. The gathering crisis was still on the horizon when Catherine finally did open the house and school in 1827. She and seven women friends began to instruct over five hundred girls in their faith and give them practical advice about how to get a job and keep it. Her advance work, calling on the parents of the Catholic children she met, resulted in a full and expanding enrollment. The four very large rooms she had stipulated in her plans for the house became the new poor schools for young girls—and with the help of Archbishop Murray of Dublin, she raised money for the support and continuance of the schools. Letters went out from her to every potential donor she could think of, all signed in the archbishop's name. In one of the earliest of those letters, Catherine spelled out her intention in building and operating the Baggot Street House:

Young tradeswomen of good character who have employment yet not sufficient means to provide safe lodging are invited to this house at night as their home—practiced in prayer and

Street beggar

meditation, prepared for the Sacraments and guarded against the dangers that surround them. You are most earnestly entreated to contribute to the support of this institution.

In another letter to a prior of a monastery Catherine explained what her House of Mercy was all about. She mentioned that it had the approval of the Archbishop of Dublin, and she outlined what she was doing at present as well as her future goals:

Very Reverend Sir

With full approbation of his grace the Archbishop, the institution in Baggot Street is to go on according to the original intention. The objects which the charity at present embrace are the daily education of hundreds of young women who sleep in the house. Objects in view—superintendence of young women employed in this house, instructing and assisting the sick poor as may hereafter be approved.

In 1828 the first House of Mercy was officially opened and blessed by the archbishop. Almost immediately, Catherine's large estate outside Dublin, Coolock House, was sold. But before leaving the site of so many good memories, she made certain that special articles of clothing and furniture dear to her were moved to the Baggot Street residence. Many are still there.

Catherine's status in the Irish Church and among the hierarchy, however, was becoming increasingly unclear now that the house was built and in operation. As long as she had lived at Coolock House, donating her time and money, she had a clearly defined place. But once Coolock was sold, she had, in a way, burned her bridges behind her. Her whole investment of time, energy and money then went into the house for the poor on Baggot Street.

"Why isn't she a religious? What is she trying to prove? Is she trying to show people up? Start something new?" These and similar questions were being asked by some members of the clergy. In nineteenth-century Ireland—and even today, to some extent—one doesn't lift one's head above the level of conformity, except in very clearly defined ways—or in battle! This was especially true for women.

When Catherine moved into this house in 1828, some of the women teaching with her in the poor schools asked if they could live with her. They began to pray together, and gradually a kind of common life sprang up. They even wore a similar type of clothing:

The first seven members and their foundress moved into a separate section of the house and began to observe greater regularity which carried over into every department. By the end of December, 1829 there were eight "sisters". Some months previously they had begun facetiously calling each other by this title.

It is easy to see why some of the Irish clergy were concerned. Catherine was not officially a member of a religious order, yet the home she had built had been approved and blessed by the archbishop. Permission had been given for her and the seven ladies helping her to have mass in the chapel—even a public mass for those who wished to attend. A chaplain had been appointed for the women and the inhabitants in the house. Collections were authorized to support the house, and the ladies attended mass and read spiritual readings together—and they even called each other "sister"! Catherine had also asked for and received permission to call her new venture The Institute of Our Blessed Lady of Mercy, at a time in history when there were no such things as secular institutes. A group of women not bound by vows but dedicated to helping the poor was unthinkable in nineteenth-century Ireland.

How could Catherine hope to avoid a collision once the house was successfully operating? She wanted "a Society of pious secular ladies who would devote themselves to the suffering and the ignorant, with liberty to return to a worldly life when they no longer felt inclined to discharge their duties." In other words, she did not want to create a religious order. The authorities on whose advice she relied had the fixed idea from the beginning that she would become a nun. She and her advisors were also at cross-purposes about how to achieve the goal they both wanted: the education of the poor and the care of the sick and homeless.

Certainly Catherine felt strongly the ambiguity of the situation and the pressure of the hierarchy. In a letter to a good friend who had been asked how the venture got started in the first place, and what were the interesting details involved, Catherine wrote rather tersely:

I would find it most difficult to write what you say Mr. Clarke (curate, St. John's Cathedral, Dublin) wishes, for the circumstances which would make it interesting could never be introduced into public discourse.

After reflecting on all this and doing some reading, I decided to go to Baggot Street again, to look at the house from a new perspective. I felt I was coming full circle, since this is where I started. But I had learned so much in the meantime that I couldn't help but see with new eyes.

Sitting next to a window on the bus, I crossed the River Liffey to where the streets got narrower and more crowded. Students from Trinity College flowed off the sidewalks and onto the streets, dressed in tweeds, hats and scarves, all busily talking. In the midst of all this activity, people and venerable buildings, stood a McDonald's restaurant, packed tight with people! One more body couldn't have fit into this latest addition to Ireland's long history.

My visit this time coincided with preparations to celebrate the 150th anniversary of the opening of Baggot Street House. It seemed as if all Ireland was celebrating. Sisters from England, Newfoundland, Australia, the United States and, of course, Ireland converged on the first House of Mercy.

Sister Finian met me at the door. She was so proud to be a part of the celebration, so excited by it all, that it was easy to get caught up in the excitement with her. We talked for a while and I asked her if I could sketch both the inside and outside of the house. Fine! And off we went in a flurry of enthusiasm to welcome excited visitors from Newfoundland.

I walked outside and around the house to get a good vantage point to sketch from, but try as I did, I could not produce a drawing of Baggot Street House that pleased me. The building seemed quite uninteresting from the outside. The original brick that Catherine had built was now covered with grey cement and the poplar trees that once stood in front of the house were gone. The house seemed boxlike and plain.

After a few attempts, I gave up trying

to sketch the building and went into the house, through a cloister and out into a lovely space of lawn bordered by a wall, which looked as if it had been built by the Vikings themselves and added onto with each successive generation.

I sat in the enclosed area and looked at that marvelous wall that seemed to have every kind of stone and style imaginable somewhere on its surface—boulders, bricks, hewn stones, cement. I had the impression that someone started to build the wall hundreds of years ago at the point where the door was, building with what he had—boulders. Successive generations added on to it, sometimes in an elaborate way. But the original wall, and gate, by comparison, still held the center of interest.

To my left was the end of the backside of Baggot Street House. The buildings I was facing had nothing to do with the first House of Mercy—except that they too faced out onto Baggot Street. As I sat and sketched, Sisters of Mercy who lived in Baggot Street House and taught in the new school to my right passed in front of me.

I was attracted to the gate in the center of the wall, wondering why it opened outward and what it opened onto. After some investigation I found that there was an alleyway on the other side of the wall, called Nun's Alley. Along that narrow alleyway Catherine and the ladies helping her would arrive in carriages pulled by galloping horses. On the other side of Nun's Alley, closer to the homes shown in the picture, were the Mews, or the places where the occupants in those houses kept their animals and carriages.

The years from 1827 to 1830 were critical for Catherine and her new venture, and the very success of the house provoked a crisis. The schools she had built and staffed were crowded with children (the number finally reaching into the thousands); the residence for young women was also crowded, with almost eighty women living in the house.

A success? Yes. But volunteers helping Catherine came and went. The one major problem was the lack of continuity in the teaching staff. There was no sense of permanence since the women helping Catherine could come and go as they wished. And many did.

The wall behind Baggot Street House

Writing to one of her sisters, Catherine said:

> In a year and a half we were joined so fast that it became a matter of general wonder. Dr. [Archbishop] Murray gave his most cordial approbation and visited frequently.

On one of the archbishop's visits he is reported to have dropped a not so subtle hint to Catherine that brought the crisis out into the open: "I did not think that founding a new order was part of your plan...really, Miss McAuley, I had no idea that a new congregation would start up this manner."

Catherine had no idea either. Confused and bewildered, she prayed over what she had heard and offered to turn over the house and the work of educating the poor to Archbishop Murray. The reason seems clear. She interpreted his remarks to mean that she should either go into a convent and start a new congregation, or return to secular life and turn the house over to a religious order—after she had given away her inheritance of 25,000 pounds!

What a choice for a woman forty-four years old. One of Catherine's biographers, speaking of this moment of crisis in her life, says:

> For one who did not like the idea of religious life, who disapproved of conventual observances, the mistress of the house on Baggot Street found herself faced with the necessity to consider both....But Almighty God had brought her by degrees to see the necessity of regular discipline and the advantages of the religious state. As the years passed, she experienced the joy of total fulfillment for which she never ceased to thank him.

Catherine's own words are somewhat less ecstatic regarding her decision to enter the religious order:

> Seeing us increase so rapidly, and all going on in the greatest order almost by itself, great anxiety was expressed to give it stability. We who began were prepared to do whatever was recommended.

In 1830, to enter a women's religious order in Ireland meant enclosure, a cloistered life with perpetual vows of poverty, chastity and obedience. It meant choir duty, strict silence and an order of the day about what should be done and when. Anything outside the cloistered life was considered of secondary importance—yet Catherine's plan was to visit the sick, which, in her mind, meant that the outside world was not of secondary but of primary importance. The works of mercy that Jesus Christ taught were to visit the sick (wherever they were) and help the poor and those in need. Coming to their aid, Catherine saw, meant life outside of the house, outside the enclosure. In fact, that is why she built the house: as a place for the poor and as a springboard for operations in the larger community.

Archbishop Daniel Murray's remark to Catherine might have been a calculated risk. He didn't know what to do with this dedicated lay person who was obviously doing the work of Christ, but wore no religious habit and did not formally belong to a congregation. And he felt the criticism by priests and religious of this woman. He wanted her in a cloister, under vows to give the life of the new institute greater stability. At least that was the message he gave her.

Some kind of compromise was made between Catherine and Archbishop Murray, but not before she did a lot of praying.

While I was in Baggot Street House, I picked up a copy of one of Catherine's prayers, one she used to say frequently. At first reading it seemed very passive, yet it was written by a very active woman who accepted challenges and took risks. Perhaps she prayed it often during this time of crisis:

My God
I am thine
For time and Eternity.
Teach me to cast myself entirely
Into the arms of Thy loving providence
With the most lively
and unlimited confidence
In Thy compassionate and tender pity.
Grant me, oh Most Merciful Redeemer,
That whatsoever Thou dost
ordain or permit
May be acceptable to me.
Take from my heart
all painful anxiety.
Suffer nothing to sadden me but sin,
Nothing to delight me
But the hope of coming to the
possession of Thee,
My God and My all,

In Thine everlasting Kingdom.
Amen.

Catherine decided to enter religious life, which meant she had to live for a year in an already-recognized religious community. Her choice was to enter a Presentation Sisters Convent in Dublin. "In September, 1830 we went . . .to George's Hill to serve a novitiate for the purpose of firmly establishing" the new congregation.

So in 1830, after the crisis, Catherine McAuley left the big house she had built on the south side of Dublin to go back to her old neighborhood on the north side of the river, not far from Abbey and Liffey Streets. She was going to a place she already knew, George's Hill Presentation Convent on North Anne Street, only blocks away from Queen Street where she lived as a young girl. She left behind her nine "sisters" and she took with her one young woman to make the year of religious training.

What convinced her finally to enter a religious order? She was confronted with a question: Would the project she had started for the poor continue during her life and, more importantly, after her death? In other words, just how much good *could* she do for Christ's poor? She was faced with the choice of institutionalizing her goals so that others could commit themselves to a similar life with the recognition and approval of the Church, or of having her house continue on as a secular institute, without being able to ask for a permanent commitment. She saw that the greatest good would be accomplished in entering and founding a religious order, where people could vow themselves in a public and lasting way. And she saw this invitation clearly coming not from the archbishop, not from within herself as she approached middle age, but from God Himself.

Nevertheless, it was a hard decision to make.

A key figure throughout her search was Dr. Michael Blake, a bishop. She consulted him about her project before any plans were drawn up. He marked out the boundaries of the property she bought and changed the plans around when they were made. He consistently supported her by sending young women who were interested in being a part of what she was doing, women who wanted to join her. He even talked to the pope about her right after the foundations of the new building were laid. The authorities in Rome were so impressed, that when a request for a new religious congregation was presented after Catherine had finished her religious training of one year, it was granted in record time.

Catherine also relied on Dr. Blake for advice: "Dr. Blake received all the ideas I had formed and I am certain he had the institute in his mind in all his communication with God." So when she was confused about which way to turn, Dr. Blake told her, "It is high time to rescue you and your associates from the anomaly of your present position; you have endured it long enough." How was she "rescued from the anomaly"? By entering the convent.

It was back to the north side of the river for Catherine. And that was where I would have to go to see the Presentation Novitiate, the place for beginners in the religious life—George's Hill. But the next day would be soon enough.

On the way back to All Hallow's College I thought of Catherine entering the novitiate. Her great fortune no longer existed; she no longer directed her own life, and other people were telling her what to do, or soon would. She was experiencing poverty in a way she had not planned.

After crossing the bridge over the river, the bus had to make a detour around the General Post Office building because of crowds of people and stalled traffic. The crowds listened to members of the IRA as they paraded and spoke. It all seemed extremely solemn. Still, I had the impression that a match would easily enkindle a flame, and I was reminded again of the Ireland of the north where Christians were fighting Christians in the name of Christ and justice. A famous theologian once said that believers killing believers, in the name of God, were responsible for much of the bloodletting throughout history.

How diametrically opposed was Catherine's action in fighting injustice and poverty.

That night, sitting in my small, faded green room, I felt dreary and emptied out. It had been a hard day's work, and my feet were hurting from miles and miles of walking. Unable to pull my thoughts together, I prayed with a pencil, trying to formulate my feelings, see them on paper. In Ireland I had found hospitality, but no friendship. I really was a stranger in this house. And one doesn't take chances with strangers. I felt very temporary. Transient. So I wrote it down:

Lord,
I am in your presence, now—
Felt strongly
In a foreign country:
A fast-moving city
Smelling
Of coal, oil and smoke,
And antiquity.

I feel bleak, alone
As I come before you this evening.
It seems as though
I am constantly forced
To go out to others,
To meet new people,
Adapt to ever-changing situations,
Witnessing ever more deeply
That one quality of life
Which disturbs me,
That it is transient!

Perhaps Catherine had similar feelings when she left Baggot Street and entered a strange new environment, a house filled with people she didn't know.

 **Chapter VIII**

Into a Convent for a Year

The following day, I again got off at O'Connell Street and walked through a fine light drizzle along the north side of the river. I had on a black, rainproofed English cap, an old jacket, faded brown pants and working shoes. On my back was my hiking bag with sketching materials, a few books and, should the rain get heavier, a raincoat.

Though I knew the general area, I didn't know exactly where George's Hill was, so I spent some time wandering around, waiting to be surprised. Finally, I turned into a side street, so narrow that two cars would have to pass each other "respectfully." On my right, halfway down the block, stood a five-story red-brick building. I passed the convent, then turned around for a better look. What a location—right in the midst of the produce markets.

Big trucks, horses pulling wagons. Foot traffic. As in all of Dublin, tremendous contrasts, with a pack of smart, young primary-school students shoving, pulling and asking me questions about America. And during all this activity, I was trying to make a drawing. The questions? Did I see such-and-such a television show? Had I ever met a movie star? Had I known John Fitzgerald Kennedy? The boys were boisterous and filled with energy, which spilled out of them as they jostled me in good humor, each and all of them craning to see better. But when the bell rang, they all disappeared, and quickly. The sisters!

The sketch shows how narrow the streets are. They were probably narrower in Catherine's time. I was looking toward Little Mary Street, a continuation of Mary Street, where Jervis Street Hospital stands. The reader is looking toward the River Liffey and across the river to the oldest section of Dublin, the area surrounding the Castle and Christ Church. On my right was the Central Fruit Company. To my left was George's Hill Convent, a formidable old building—a four-story fortress, sur-

George's Hill Presentation Convent

rounded by tall black spikes. Dublin is a city of walls, and this building is no exception. A black iron gate opened into a narrow path that led to the entrance of the convent, built in 1794, when Cathreine, at age eight, lived close by. She certainly would have remembered seeing and hearing about this building, because it was talked about—a *convent* of nuns!

I rang the doorbell and waited patiently in the rain. A pretty young sister came to the door, gave me a careful look and asked noncommittally, "Yes?"

I asked her if her superior was at home—not the kind of question she would expect from someone looking for a handout. She was somewhat taken aback, but just for an instant. Then, with a half-smile, as though I had won a reprieve by a clever argument and she were acknowledging it, she said, "Well, now, maybe. It depends upon your business." The Irish have a quick wit and are rarely at a loss for words.

I told her that I was a Catholic priest and that I was doing a book on Catherine McAuley. As soon as I said "priest" the door opened wide.

Amazing trust. I was ushered into an elaborately furnished guest dining room. Bells were rung. Sisters began moving around within the house. And tea appeared, good strong black tea, served with sweets.

Despite the reception, I felt very much out of place in the guest room because of the way I was dressed. But if the Sisters of the Presentation noticed it, they didn't show it, insisting that I sit at the table, covered with fine linen, and enjoy my tea. And were they gracious! I met the superior, the former superior, the oldest sister in the house, the house historian and, finally, the community, in that order.

Catherine entered this community in September, 1830. Three months later she was clothed in the habit of the Presentation Order. A year later, she took her vows. All this recorded in the convent records:

Sister Catherine, daughter of James McAuley and Eleanor Conway was born in the parish of Glasnevin, Diocese of Dublin, was baptized and confirmed. She entered this convent on the 8th of September 1830, took the habit of this congregation on the

9th of December 1830 being 44 years of age. She made her profession on the 12th day of December 1831 in the chapel of this Convent of the Presentation, with permission and in the presence of Most Rev. Father in God, Daniel Murray, Lord Archbishop of Dublin.

After tea I was given a tour of the house, and I could see the different levels of its history in the sections that had been added on since 1794. When the tour was finished, I asked to see the room Catherine had lived in for a year. I walked up five flights of stairs, down a corridor and into a kind of annex that contained three rooms. The end room had been Catherine's during her one year of training, a bright room looked out over the city. But, of course, it was not so bright during her time; the wallpaper certainly did not have flowers on it when she entered.

Catherine's room was one of three private rooms that opened out into a corridor separated again from the main corridor at the head of the stairs by a wall. In each room was a small glass window over the door to insure that novices were in bed and, literally, not burning the midnight oil. Light was provided by a sister who came around at dusk with a match or candle and lighted each candle of the sisters. One look at the little window above the door would tell the superior if any of the young sisters were breaking the rule, but I couldn't even imagine the possibility of such a thing in those days.

The room now belongs to Sister Bernadette, a sharp, bright, humorous woman who was very gracious about letting me use her bedroom. I did a sketch of it, positioning myself in the corridor and looking through the half-opened door. Just above Sister Bernadette's bed was a picture of the lady from Dublin, Catherine McAuley.

After I finished the sketch, I looked out the window that faced the Apothecaries Hall and the streets on which Catherine grew up. I thought to myself that, here in this room, she wasn't too far from home. All she had to do was look out the window. But when I suggested this to Sister Bernadette, she laughed and replied that in those days the windows were frosted and kept shut—and shuttered! Wooden panels closed over the glass and heavy, coarse

89

Catherine McCauley's room at George's Hill Convent

cloth drapes hung over the wooden panels. How had Catherine breathed? Suddenly the cheerful room, sans window, flowery wallpaper and electric lights, became in my mind a dark compartment. Still, I was fascinated with what I could see looking out the window, and I thought that perhaps Catherine peeked once in a while when no one was looking. I got down on the floor. The window was constructed in such a way that it couldn't be opened except part way from the top and the bottom. Sitting on the floor was too low. I needed something to sit on to have a clear, unobstructed view of the city. Nearby was Sister's kneeler, a small wooden step that some people use to pray. It did not make a very good chair, but it was better than not sitting at all. So I sat, crouched over—a very uncomfortable position—sketching what I thought Catherine saw, at least once or twice, looking out the window that faces the distant O'Connell Street.

Just below the window was a cross that surmounted the chapel she took her vows in. To the left, during her time, was the big Newgate Prison; to the right, the Jervis Street Hospital; and straight ahead, the Apothecaries Hall.

What struck me as I looked out the window was the proximity of these key places in her life. She was familiar with poverty, crime and sickness from the time she moved into the city. They surrounded her. She couldn't escape them. It wasn't unusual, then, that the Order of Sisters she established tended toward the care of the sick and dispossessed from the very beginning. God prepared her for this work through His providence. And that providence was shown, or revealed, by the surroundings in which she lived and the natural inclinations that she had within her, touched by Grace. Even the very determined direction of Archbishop Murray revealed that providence.

While I was doing the picture, one of the older sisters, very excited that I was doing a book on Catherine that would include her stay at George's Hill Convent, kept running up and down the four flights of stairs to keep track of the progress of the sketch. She felt that she was witnessing a historic moment. All I felt was the desire to see the area she grew up in and through which God spoke to her, and get a good sketch of it. But thank God for other people's excitement.

From this bird's eye view of a room, I descended the four flights of stairs, went outside the house and, with two Presentation Sisters leading the way, passed through a heavy, black, spiked gate at the bottom of a damp cement staircase. We went into an underground crypt. The walls were rough, unevenly textured and curved at the ceiling, as though someone had scooped them out hundreds of years ago and then painted them chalk-white year after year. Along the walls were the resting places of the women who had been living upstairs.

As I walked through the crypt, looking at the names and dates of the sisters who had died, I visualized in my mind the funeral ceremony that took place whenever there was a death: flickering candles, leaping shadows and the mournful sound of the *Te Deum*. What a place for a meditation on the shortness of life.

Coming out of the crypt was like acting out the Resurrection, coming up from the world of the dead. And Catherine had made the same journey I did, perhaps a number of times.

What a year this must have been for her in this house. At age forty-four, she was put into the hands of a very rigid novice mistress, who wanted to make sure that Catherine understood the place of humiliation and penance in the religious life. It is not hard to imagine how a strict novice mistress might act, knowing she was training a future novice mistress—and foundress—for, after her year at George's Hill, Catherine was to take her vows and return to Baggot Street to train her own sisters in the new congregation that would be called the Sisters of Mercy. She would become a novice mistress herself.

How did she take to life in this convent during this year? According to one of her biographers, "She would not have remained overnight except that she realized the importance of her work." Her training was rigorous and rigidly enforced. By twentieth-century standards, the training seems irrational. For along with the spiritual and intellectual training were included "penances" designed to break, or at least very effectively mold, her will:

Looking out Catherine's window

On one occasion when she remained a few minutes beyond the specific time with her young relatives (who were visiting her), Catherine McAuley and Teresa Byrne, ages eleven and nine, her Mistress of Novices commanded her to kneel with her arms extended at the end of the Sister's dining room and then ''forgot'' her for several hours. When the children visited her again, she was told to read to them from the Imitation of Christ by Thomas Kempis, but not to talk to them. Upon their final visit, the Mistress entered and reproved her so severely in their presence that the girls begged Catherine to return home with them.

Later that day, I had dinner with the assembled community in the dining room. I sat at the head of a rectangle of tables, with the sisters, dressed in long habits down to their ankles, on both sides and in front of me. I learned that George's Hill was the only Presentation Convent in the world where, until recently, a woman could enter with the intention of residing there until death. The superior, a charming woman who knew how to be a superior, was well on her way to doing that. She had lived there for forty years.

Our conversation at dinner went from the discoveries being made of the original Viking town on Wood Quay, next to the river, to the rigid novice mistress in charge of Catherine McAuley. The sisters were intellectually stimulating, charming and gracious. While eating and listening, I observed that these sisters knew each other well. The conversation, the reaction to what some sister said, the general response of laughter to something funny—all was like a well-orchestrated piece of music. That they had lived with each other for a long time was evident in the way one deferred to the other or picked up a loose end of the string of conversation and continued weaving it into something all could share in.

After dinner I was shown a magnificent crown of thorns with long, slender, almost perfect spines, and I was told this was an exact replica of the crown of thorns that Christ wore. The crown was housed in a bell glass jar. When I asked the sisters how they knew for certain that it was an *exact* replica of Christ's crown, I got an uncomprehending stare, as though I had suddenly turned into an infidel right before their eyes. We then visited the chapel in which Catherine took her vows fifteen months after entering the convent, on December 12, 1831.

Her vow formula, or the act of profession that she made on that day, is interesting in that it reveals she was vowing her life in the congregation of the Sisters of Mercy (not yet officially recognized), but according to the rules and constitution of the Presentation Order, since she was the first Sister of Mercy and there was still no such congregation when she took her vows:

In the name of Our Lord Jesus Christ and under the protection of his Blessed Mother, I, Catherine McAuley, called in religion Sister Mary Catherine, do vow perpetual poverty, chastity, and obedience, and to preserve until the end of my life in the congregation called the Sisters of Mercy, established for the visitation of the sick, poor, and charitable instruction of poor females according to the rules and constitutions of the Presentation Order, subject to such alterations as shall be approved by the Archbishop, you, my Lord and most Reverend Father in God, Daniel Murray, Archbishop of this Diocese...in the year of Our Lord, one thousand eight hundred and thirty-one on this twelfth day of December.

On the inside of her vow ring were inscribed these words: *Fiat Voluntas Tua,* "may your will be done"—the response of Mary to what was incomprehensible in her life.

She took her vows on the twelfth of December, and on the same day, without even waiting for a prepared breakfast, she was back at Baggot Street.

It was eight years before Catherine returned to George's Hill. The scene of some painful humiliations hadn't changed that much, but the pain had been forgotten, and with a burst of good humor, she wrote to a woman she had a deep friendship with, sister Mary Francis Warde:

We visited our old George's Hill—they were delighted, and so was I—said I would kiss the chairs and tables (a reference to practices of penance), but by some mistake I kissed a grand new chair in the parlor; however, I managed as ducky Mary Quin used (your mother)—I took it back and brought it up to the old rush chair I used to sit on in the noviceship.

She could laugh about it eight years later.

When she returned to Baggot Street, the spirits of the group waiting for her picked up and showed in the reception they gave her. Her companions, her relatives, women living in the house and many young girls who were being cared for were all there. But the reception wasn't all joy, for the regular affairs of the house were in a state of chaos. Because of overwork and lack of her guidance, some of her companions, including her niece, were sick. One yound lady had even died from exhaustion. They had missed Catherine.

The day after her return, Archbishop Murray appointed her as "Reverend Mother." She was now the official foundress and superior of the new congregation. Young women could join with her and live out a vowed life, and they did, with Catherine as their novice mistress. It was her turn to take what she had learned—some of which she had to unlearn—together with what she knew to be the spirit of mercy, and teach the beginner. She was glad to get away from George's Hill and be back with her own.

It was time for me, also, to leave George's Hill since the day was reaching toward dusk. I thanked the sisters for their hospitality and promised I would return should I get the chance. I walked to the bus and started out of Dublin. It was almost dark when I reached my stop-off point, The Cat and Cage Pub, and as I walked along the wall bordering All Hallows, listening to the night sounds, I felt content with the day's work.

When I got to the college, I went into the kitchen for a cup of coffee. The night secretary and the two boys were watching television. Again there was a knock on the door leading to the courtyard, and again the occupants in the kitchen acted out the nightly ritual of surreptitiously bringing out coffee and food to Kevin, waiting in the cold outside.

 # Chapter IX

A New Beginning and an End

Later on in the week I returned to Baggot Street House, only this time I went by way of what once was called the most beautiful park in all of Ireland: Merrion Square. The park, which is right around the block from Baggot Street House, is surrounded by trees, wide, open streets and Georgian buildings decorated with iron grillwork and ornate balconies. Shining brass was everywhere I looked, and the air was cold enough to frost my breath—a crystal morning! The streets were all but empty, so I sketched the scene.

In the nineteenth century this square was a place for wealthy and talented people: poets, artists and statesmen. Daniel O'Connell, the Liberator and later Lord Mayor of Dublin, lived here. An orator who could hold thousands spellbound, his speech about the Sisters of Mercy caused a minor sensation and an influx of young women into the congregation. Catherine retold part of his talk to a friend, and her comments are an insight into nineteenth century Irish rhetoric as well as the effect the work of the new congregation was having on Dubliners:

Did you hear what a handsome tribute of regard Mr. O'Connell paid the Sisters of Mercy in his speech at Carrick? It is bringing them quite into fashion. As a test of my humility I have it in my desk to look at occasionally, and will copy it for you.

"No country on the face of the earth is like Ireland. Look at the fairest portion of creation (women) educated and possessing all the virtues that adorn and endear life, forsaking their homes and families, and friends—entering a convent in the morning of their days, to devote long lives to piety and the promotion of virtue. Look at the Sisters of Mercy (hear hear) wrapped in their long black cloaks. They are seen gliding along the streets in their humble attire, while a slight glance at the foot shows the

Merrion Square

accomplished lady. (cheers) Thus they go forth, not for amusement or delight; no. They are hastening to the lone couch of some sick fellow-creature, fast sinking into the grave with none to comfort, none to soothe; they come with love and consolation, and by their prayers, bring down the blessings of God on the dying sinner, on themselves, and on their community. (great cheering) Oh, such a country is too good to continue in slavery. (immense cheering)...''

The foot has afforded great amusement...each claiming for her own foot the compliment paid to all... Give my most affectionate love to each. All unite in love to you. Your attached

M.C. McAuley

The new congregation started to grow, and the work of the sisters made a profound impression. In addition to teaching in what was called the poor schools, the sisters visited the hospitals to help the sick and the dying. They sought out the poor wherever they could find them—in the alleys and the smoky lanes, up into attics and down into cellars, into prisons, workhouses—

wherever the poor and the sick were, the sisters went. Daniel O'Connell's speech about them was not simply a piece of rhetoric. It was a statement of truth of what the Sisters of Mercy were all about: women who came to the aid of the disadvantaged, as Jesus Christ had.

Catherine was very explicit about the qualities she hoped to find, or develop, in the young women applying for admission. To a parish priest who wanted to know what these qualities were, she wrote:

In compliance with your desire, Rev. Sir, I shall submit what seems "generally" requisite for a "Sister of Mercy." Besides an ardent desire to be united to God, and serve the poor, she must feel a particular interest for the sick and dying, otherwise the duty of visiting them would soon become exceedingly toilsome.

Sister Finian met me again at the door of Baggot Street House. I asked her where the poor schools were located in the original plans of the building, and she was only too glad to show me. We went to one of the wings, up three stories and into what were once over-sized rooms where the children were taught. Nearby were the dormitories where those who needed shelter stayed.

The dormitories and classrooms were now painted a warm color. Their appearance belied their past, for I later saw faded, brown pictures taken in the 1800s of the many young girls learning trades and studying under the watchful eyes of the sisters. The children all looked very serious. Life was then, as it still is for most of the world's inhabitants, a serious, harsh business. That seriousness was reflected in both the faces of the students and their teachers.

Life was harsh for the sisters, with constant work and religious exercises each day. This was the *revised* order of the day, and it was *closely* followed:

5:00 A.M.	—Rise
7:00	—Office and meditation over
7:15	—Mass
8:15	—Breakfast
9:00	—Lecture for all
9:30	—Visiting the sick or teaching
11:45	—Examination of conscience in chapel
12:00	—Prayers; resume work
3:00 P.M.	— Dinner for House of Mercy inhabitants
4:00	—Dinner for sisters
5:00	—Vespers, followed by lecture
6:45	—Visit to chapel
7:00	—Tea, followed by recreation
9:00	—General exam, points, litany. . . rest

There was little room for laziness in such a schedule. The revision came about because too many of the young sisters were getting sick—not from overwork, but from the practice of extreme poverty, lack of sufficient recreation and not enough food. Some of the rigorousness of her noviate training showed up when Catherine first started teaching her young companions.

Because so many of the women were getting sick, a doctor was called in to determine why:

Sir Philip Crampton, Surgeon General, was summoned, and after

The Liberator, Daniel O'Connell

careful inquiry, found the lack of food and the long hours of labor responsible for the poor health of many. He insisted that they have better meat and drink: he recommended that beer be made available to them. Because he considered the silence observed at meals was unwholesome, more recreation was given at mealtime.

Each day Catherine taught the sisters and sent them out to work with the sick and poor. At first they were shocked by the reaction of the poor, their language and their refusal to accept help. When the young sisters, who had come from good homes, complained to Catherine, she replied: "The wealthy have generally but a very limited knowledge of the actual privations of the poor, and even you yourselves have but lately gained any information on the suject."

But they did gain that information rapidly when a cholera epidemic broke out in Ireland a year after Catherine returned from George's Hill. At one point the estimated death toll was as high as six hundred people a day. The average uneducated person was terrified. Many people believed life was over as soon as anyone entered the doors of a hospital, and some were even convinced that the doctors were murdering the patients there.

In such a context of fear and suspicion it was difficult for the doctors to be of any help to the masses of afflicted people. Realizing this, the Dublin Board of Health asked the sisters to take over a hospital on Townsend Street to care for the victims. They agreed, and when people saw the sisters administer the medicine and act as nurses, the fear and suspicion vanished.

The sisters were not afraid of death. In fact, a desire to minister to those dying was one of the qualities Catherine looked for in a woman seeking entrance. Their lack of fear gave them an enormous power in helping the sick, for in the sisters' minds, death was related to Someone higher, deeper and more lasting: God and His love and mercy. So death wasn't final. They communicated this belief and also provided medical help, in much the same way as Mother Theresa does to the derelicts on the streets of Calcutta. Perhaps the term "angel of mercy" came about during the cholera epidemic in 1832, when Catherine and her companions administered to the sick and dying in the Townsend Street hospital.

What a toll this ministry was to take on the new group. During the first seven years of the new congregation's life, fifteen young women died, none over twenty-three years old. Not all of their deaths were from exhaustion. They also succumbed to disease: tuberculosis, typhoid fever and cholera claimed their lives as they had the lives of thousands of others in Catherine's time.

It is difficult to comprehend that simple precautions for avoiding disease were either unknown or not taken in that pre-pasteurization age: well-water was often contaminated, sewage disposal often neglected. The way milk was purified for human consumption says much about the state of medicine and health, as well as the spread of disease. The following is a description of the process that was common then:

To satisfy me the engine (for purification) was brought to us which was a round thing made from the bark of a birch tree, of a conical figure, and stuffed with clean straw or grass, and through this they let their milk run, by which the hairs and dirt are separated from it.

Despite the sickness and death of so many of her young companions, despite poverty and opposition, Catherine remained optimistic, trusting that she was doing God's work. She could even overlook her own faults. Years later she said of the beginning:

There has been a most marked Providential Guidance which the want of prudence, vigilance, or judgement has not impeded, and it is here that we can most clearly see the designs of God. I could mark circumstances calculated to defeat it [the congregation] at once, but nothing injurious in itself has done any injury. . .The loss of property has been supplied, the death of the most valuable Sisters passed away as of no consequence. The alarm that was spread by such repeated deaths did not prevent others crowding in, in short, it evidently was to go on, and surmount all obstacles, many of which were great indeed, preceding from causes within and without.

For three years, from 1831 to 1834, Catherine and Archbishop Murray worked together to establish the guiding rules and constitutions of the new order, which would ideally spell out the order's spirit. By 1834 they were finished and sent to Rome for approval.

Sister Finian showed me a copy of the original rules, and I looked them over carefully. I was struck by the difference between Catherine's handwriting and the archbishop's. Hers was carefully defined, firm, determined and practical; she spelled out clearly what she saw as the spirit of the order in measured, orderly handwriting. And crossing out her writing, correcting it, were the great scrawls of Archbishop Murray. The image that came to my mind was that of a giant dirt-mover, plowing its way into the hillside. And some of his corrections seemed arbitrary, as though he felt he had to be correcting something. So down came the pen with bold strokes, changing not the idea, at times, but the wording.

Along with teaching, visiting the sick and writing the constitutions, Catherine discovered between 1835 and 1841 what happens to foundresses of new and needed congregations: requests for more Houses of Mercy. During those seven years, Catherine founded thirteen new houses. She not only started them, but visited them regularly (while continuing to administer Baggot Street House) and kept a constant correspondence going with the sisters of each new foundation.

It was Catherine's personal contact, her love and affection for each of her sisters, that was the key to the congregation's growth. This quality is quite evident in a letter of Catherine's to a young girl entering the congregation. Mary Delamere lived in Tullamore, fifty-eight miles west of Dublin, where the first House of Mercy outside of Dublin was established in 1836.

A foundation was a major event involving not only extensive preparation, but days of travel by boat and carriage, meetings with the local clergy, setting up the house and consulting with young women who wished to join. In 1836 Catherine and two other sisters, one of whom was ready to pronounce vows, sailed west by flyboat on the Grand Canal to Tullamore.

The pastor of the church, a good-sized crowd who had heard of the Sisters of Mercy and some young women who wanted to join greeted Catherine and her sisters. It was a celebration. With an eye to impressing people with the right kind of witnessing, Catherine decided that the young novice ready to pronounce vows should do so publicly in church, a first of its kind in Tullamore. The church was filled, the people deeply impressed.

One of the women most impressed was Mary Delamere. Two weeks after having met and talked with Catherine, she decided to apply for entrance. Three months later she was formally received, and Catherine, who had returned to Dublin, came back for the reception. A month before she did, however, she wrote a letter to the young woman that reveals the secret of the closeness that knitted the Sisters of Mercy together:

My Dear Sr. Mary,

It has given me great pleasure to find you are so happy, and I really long for the time we are to meet again, please God. But the good Mother Superior will not have equal reason to rejoice, for I am determined not to behave well, and you must join me.

If I write to mention the day we propose going, you might contrive to put the clock out of order, though that would almost be a pity. By some means we must have until ten o'clock every night, not a moment's silence until we are asleep—not to be disturbed till we awake. Take care to have the key of the cross-door, and when those who are not so happily disposed, go into choir, we can lock them in until breakfast....Of one thing, however, I am sure and seriously so, that I seldom look forward to any change in this world as I do to our meeting...

Believe me Sr. Mary with
 Sincere affection, etc., etc.,
  M. C. McAuley

Remember me to your Mamma.

The affection displayed in this letter shows why the deaths of her young sisters touched her personally. She knew them; she had come to love them. But also because in some cases there were deep, strong bonds of relationship. Both her nieces, Theresa and Catherine, died young as Sisters of

Mercy, breaking Catherine's heart. The two girls were the daughters of her sister Mary. Theresa died in 1833 and Catherine in 1837.

Young Catherine's sickness, which her aunt could see was fatal, must have been a focal point for many of the reversals that the foundress experienced in the years 1837-1840: legal troubles with one of the pastors in whose parish a House of Mercy had been established; the loss of a chaplain for the House of Mercy on Baggot Street; and now the impending loss of her niece.

She is so much changed [she wrote of her niece] . . . this morning I fell down the second flight of stairs. My side is quite sore, but if ever so well able, I could not leave my poor child.

Two weeks later she wrote: "Our innocent little Catherine is out of this miserable world. . . . She suffered very little, thanks be to God."

But in a personal vein she confessed to her close friend, Frances Warde, the effect of her nieces' deaths on her: "I have suffered more than usual with my old pain of sorrow and anxiety. My stomach has been very ill."

Despite the deaths of the sisters and the new foundations, the congregation continued to grow. And despite Catherine's sorrow and anxiety, her faith in God never wavered. She was convinced from the beginning that God was in the works of mercy that she and her companions were doing. She said with some asperity when asked about her conviction:

We now have gone beyond 100 in number, and the desire to join seems rather to increase, though it was thought the foundations would retard it, it seems to be quite otherwise. . . .The alarm that was spread by such repeated deaths did not prevent others crowding in, in short, it evidently was to go on.

By the year 1838 there were eight Houses of Mercy. Requests for more foundations and sisters continued coming in, even from outside Ireland. When possible, each new foundation consisted of a convent or house for the sisters, to which was often adjoined a house for orphans, widows, servants or distressed girls. The growing network of Sisters of Mercy was directed from

Baggot Street, which was—and still is to some extent—home base for the Mercy Sisters around the world.

As Catherine got older, her activity increased—hardly something she would have envisioned while riding horses and walking the vast expanses of lawn at Coolock House. She wrote what she felt about her increase in activity as the foundations multiplied:

We have a striking example before us of the power of exercising unwearied efforts of mind and body, in the perpetual movements of the steam carriages which seem just passing our window.

Quite a picture: Catherine at her desk writing; the noise of the steam engine coming down the street; Catherine getting up to look at it. In the effortless motion of the machine she could see the whole of the technological revolution—and the dilemma too: how to harness the energy man is capable of creating, to do what is good and to create a new world. Her answer, it seems, was to imitate the steam engine; but eventually that road took an enormous toll. Writing a bit later in the same year, she wasn't quite as euphoric:

We are near a stop—I should say a full stop. Hands and feet are plentiful enough, but the heads are nearly gone. Get all the prayers you can that we may get well through this business.

The business that Catherine wanted to get through was simply the year 1838—for two reasons, both of them connected with the clergy, and both, it seems, motivated by jealousy and distrust. The cause of the jealousy and distrust may have been the fact that, although Catherine's congregation had been approved, the final rules and constitutions had not. They were still going back and forth between Dublin and Rome. They were not finally approved until 1841, the year of her death. During the years 1834-1841, some members of the clergy adopted a wait-and-see approach toward her status in Rome—which soon became condescending. They saw her congregation as a flash in the pan, an eccentric idea of a rich old lady and not a bona fide religious congregation approved by the Church. And their attitude persisted despite the obvious success of the sisters' activities.

This attitude of distrust was certainly at work when the pastor of the local parish for Baggot Street House refused point-blank to supply a chaplain for the house and the people who lived there when the regular chaplain, after seven years of service, had gone to Africa as a missionary. The pastor, Dean Meyler, refused to designate one man who could be chaplain, one the sisters could get to know and trust. Instead he demanded the payment of fifty pounds a year for whoever happened to be free to say mass for the sisters or hear their confessions. It could be a different priest each time, in other words. She pleaded to a friend:

Will you relieve me from the distressing business about the chaplain. It is constantly before me, and makes me dread going home. I know it is not possible for me to have any more argument with Dr. Meyler without extreme aggravation....Will you not, my dear, speak to Mr. Lynch (the curate) and say, in a most decided manner, that we require a chaplain to the house, and cannot nor will not call on any of the parish clergymen to attend the institution. This will imply that no salary will be given. You may add that Mr. Armstrong [a priest and close friend and confidant of Catherine's who died in 1828 and was instrumental in all her plans] told me it would be injurious, indeed, he said if we were a religious community it could not be attempted, and he was deeply afflicted on his deathbed that we were not so established.

Dean Meyler was repeating what had happened earlier in 1828 before Catherine entered the novitiate at George's Hill, when the pastor, Father Kelly, who did not like Catherine and thought she was an upstart, refused to send a chaplain to the house for mass and confessions. Catherine, faced with the same possibility again, recalled her determination to obtain a chaplain from Father Meyler or do without one:

Mr. Kelly who was parish priest... kept us a year and a half walking to Clarendon Street [for mass] every day—poor women and children...I would rather do so again than consent to it. We will all find room in Westland Row (St. Andrew Church).

Were the congregation fully approved in its rules and constitutions, Dean Meyler would not have hesitated to send a chaplain.

There were a lot of people in Baggot Street House—girls, orphans, widows, sisters—and each day for the three years left for Catherine, she, or the woman in charge when she was absent, got all the children up, walked a mile to the church on Westland Row and back during snow, rain and good weather. The pastor refused to think of any other arrangement. And whatever the arrangement, he wanted fifty pounds for it:

> We get an occasional charitable mass and never go out on very wet mornings. I am sure Dr. Meyler would wish the matter settled according to his own plan. We would have at least three priests and never know who to call on as friend or chaplain, and for this we must pay or promise to pay 50 pounds per annum, which we really have not. . . . I offered 40 pounds to Dr. Meyler, and I now believe it is well it was rejected.

Still she could add: "I am not unhappy, thanks be to God, nor do I see any disedification likely to arise from this matter."

Not having a chaplain for Baggot Street House was a painful hardship. Add to this the exertion spent on the new foundations, the sadness over her nieces' deaths and the ambiguity of her standing with Rome. It is easy to see why 1838 was a trying year for Catherine. But there was still one other source of pain, a lawsuit brought against her by a priest in whose parish she had established a House of Mercy. These circumstances forced one of her few written expressions of anger:

> Pray fervently for me, that God may remove all bitterness far from me. I can hardly think of what has been done to me without resentment. May God forgive me, and make me truly humble before He calls me into His presence.

I went back into the room in which Catherine died and looked at her desk where many letters had been written. Letters of relief, joy, anger and sadness, but especially letters of encouragement to her overworked sisters as the demands for new houses continued.

Catherine herself was weighed down by the distrust of the clergy and her failing health. After returning from a trip in 1840, she wrote to a friend:

Thank God, I am at rest again. I think the name of another foundation would make me sick but the Sisters say I would get up again. Indeed, the thought of one at present would greatly distress me. On the late occasion I travelled a hundred miles a day (stage coach) which is very fatiguing except on railroads.

And she did get up again.

Catherine and the Sisters of Mercy went from Dublin to Kingstown in 1838, to Tullamore in 1837, Booters-town and Limerick in 1838 and Naas in 1839. Then they skipped over to London in the same year, traveled to Galway in 1840, Wexford and Birr the same year and Birmingham in 1841, the year of her death. And in each place a new House of Mercy came into existence—all in seven years. She must have felt like a spider trying to keep the center of the web supported as the strands radiated out from that center. A bishop of the time said of the new order:

The Order of Mercy must prosper. All its members are willing to travel hundreds of miles to aid, counsel, and support each other, and this is their established practice. It cannot fail, while such affectionate interest is manifested.

Catherine's affection for her sisters and her work as well as her deep trust in God that He would draw good out of evil, easily won out over her bitterness about the chaplain and the lawsuit.

In 1840 Catherine and four other sisters traveled by boat and mail coach to a town of four thousand people. The town, Birr, was well-named, for it was caught in the middle of a severe cold spell. She had been invited to open a House of Mercy, and as usual she accompanied those who would be in charge. When she arrived with the other sisters, the pastor of the church spoke to his congregation, introducing them. They had heard about the sisters and welcomed them, for the town itself had been split into factions by the defection of a Catholic priest:

My dear people, I have a present to make you. I have a New Year's gift for you, the most gratifying that a pastor could have. I present you the Sisters of Mercy, who by their example and pious instructions will draw upon our town the blessings of heaven.

Reflecting on the pastor's speech—and her remarks certainly show that Catherine had changed considerably from the time of her novitiate and the early days of "no talking at meals, nor recreation"—she wrote to a friend: "We had great laughing at breakfast, saying he might have tried us a little longer, not to make a present of us so soon." Her affection and good humor were still intact.

The severe cold spell, and the fact that the house the sisters lived in was right next to the river and therefore damp, was Catherine's undoing. Over and over again she mentions that she was deeply affected by the cold:

My dear Sr. Mary Cecilia,

Here we are surrounded by New-foundland ice, obliged to keep hot turf under the butter to enable us to cut it. Tell Sr. M. Francis I am obliged to take hold of some person to keep me up.

Sr. Mary Rose and I walked one mile and a half yesterday, in all the snow, to visit an unfortunate family.

The work of visiting the sick, helping the poor and instructing those who needed it went on despite the weather. In the same letter to Sister Mary she mentions:

All my wardrobe is washing. I came home yesterday with at least half a yard of deep mud, melted snow, and I have not a cold in my head—I was out five hours. Hurrah for foundations, makes the old young and the young merry.

She may have felt young, but the cold was doing its work on her:

With all around me covered with snow, and my poor fingers petrified, I will endeavor to write a few lines to you...my fingers are cold and stiff. ...I am so frozen, so petrified with cold that I can scarcely hold the pen ...I feel the frost most acutely in my right side from my hip to my ankle. I have put on a great flannel bandage with camphorated spirit, and trust in God it will, like a dear old acquaintance, carry me safe back.

When Catherine returned by coach

from the foundation at Birr, in February, 1841, she joked about her feeling sick:

I could scarcely do justice in description to the kindness of the two coachmen. The first, from the time we left Birr, at every stage was very compassionate to me, offering to carry me into the Inns, to get to a fire, really uneasy about me. When changing (coaches) he recommended me to the second who was equally kind, and neither sought any payment. I mention this as I never met any thing of the sort before. When we arrived in Dublin, my "weak side" was stiff and I was quite shrunk in size. A car was waiting for me, with a very small man as a driver. The good coach man said, "Is this little man come for this little woman?"

"Yes."

"Oh, then I am glad. She's lost with cold and hunger."

Something more than a surface sickness had taken hold of Catherine. She eventually died from what she had caught at Birr. And from this point on, her illness becomes a subject of humor in her letters, but also of concern: "I have been anxious to write, but my old cough has made me nervous that I could not nor cannot now write distinctly." To her good friend Mary Francis Warde she confesses that she expects the sickness will be with her until death:

My dearest Sr. Mary Francis

I am sorry to find by your letter this morning that they (the Sisters) are saying too much about my loss of health. My rather new visitant, a cough, has been with me very constantly since the first Sunday after my return. To please my kind tormentors, I took one large bottle of medicine and put on a small blister, from which I (for want of faith perhaps) did not receive any benefit. I am now doctoring myself as I have Sr. Theresa. Very warm flannel entire dress, mellow barley water, old fashioned sugar candy, a little Hippo at night, and I think Mr. Time taken into account I am doing very well. I do think that a cough has made a resting place with me, and will be no unusual visitor in future. I am now going to hide from the doctor who has gone up to the four influenza patients.

"Blisters, old fashioned sugar candy, and mellow barley water" are hardly conducive to curing tuberculosis, but the cure used by Catherine certainly reveals the primitive state of medicine in 1840.

In one sense the cure was unimportant, for she had an incredibly strong belief that no matter what happened God was in it—even her own illness. So she achieved a real distance from it by making light of it. Only a person in touch with life, who could see within it more than life, could afford a sense of humor.

In 1841, the year of Catherine's death, the constitutions and rules of the new order were finally and formally approved by Rome, and the young became even more confident in entering. Baggot Street House was soon filled with women who wanted to follow Catherine McAuley's way of life; and even though sisters were being sent out on missions as soon as they were ready, there was hardly any room left. During a lull, when thirteen sisters were about to be missioned away from the house, Catherine wrote to a friend of hers:

We shall soon have a very thin house, if God is not pleased to send us a new batch. If four go to Newfoundland, and nine to Birmingham, thirteen vacant cells will be a curiosity here. This will be a relief to my poor little house-steward, Sr. M. Teresa (the less), who has often been perplexed to make out a bed, so much so, that I used to try to avoid her when an addition was on the way. We were sure to hear something like the following dialogue:

"Reverend Mother, I hear there's another Sister coming?"

"Yes, have you any objections?"

"Where is she to sleep?"

"In my lap."

"Oh, I declare, Reverend Mother, it is impossible."

Catherine had accomplished a great deal in the ten years of the new order's existence, and all the good she accomplished was furthered and animated by her many letters, most of them filled with affection, good humor and practical advice. Her hopes for the future were placed in God and in her sisters, who were like floating anchors that stabilize a ship even in the stormy

117

weather and allow it to ride the sea. From her desk top, letter after letter went out to different parts of the country, each bearing the unmistakable mark of friendship:

I have come back to my old corner to write to you after all are gone to bed; we are exactly as you left us. We expect a postulant, not twenty yet, very pleasing and very musical. It is past ten; the fire is out, and the windows are making an awful noise; so I must have done.

In fact, the fire *was* almost out. And Catherine sensed that herself. She was suffering from exhaustion. Her stomach was upset, and she could take only baby food for a while. Her mouth was infected, and her arm broken from an accident. She had an ominous cough that wouldn't go away. Still, she continued her incessant pace right up until the end.

Shortly before her death, she wrote on the constant hazards of traveling:

I am anxious to write to you from my strange habitation. How many new beds have I rested in! When I awake in the morning, I ask myself where I am; and, on the last two or three foundations, I could not recollect for some moments.

Four months later, Catherine knew for certain that she was going to die, and she kept it a secret, to all appearances functioning as usual. In November, 1841, she was so sick that she was anointed in her room and mass was celebrated.

In this room she died. Nearly a century and a half later, I sat on the chaise lounge against the wall. In front of me were her desk, an inkwell, her cross— the one she was holding when she died—her letter box and two more pieces of furniture from Coolock House. The chair on the left was, according to Sister Finian, the one she used while teaching the young sisters after she returned from George's Hill Convent. To the right of the letter box was a knitting basket. Just above the finely carved chair, but out of sight, was the picture of Mr. William Callaghan.

I noticed that the brass fittings on the letter box had been tampered with, forced open. Sister Finian explained that a few nights earlier a man had broken into the house, through a stained glass window. I couldn't even picture such a thing happening in Ireland. Not only did he break in, but he wandered around the corridors and walked up the steps to this room, entering it and going over to the letter box. Forcing it open and finding nothing, he took the cross. Then holding it aloft, he opened the door to one of the sister's room. Terrified, she hid behind the door. In walked the intruder, holding the cross on high and shouting out, "Don't be afraid, I am a man of God!" The police were right behind him. They took the "man of God" down to the massive, gray police station opposite Trinity College and booked him, "drunk."

The next day the sisters decided to not only replace the stained glass window, but to lace it with protective bars of steel.

As Catherine lay dying in this room, her niece came close to her. Catherine breathed out, "Kiss me, my heart, then go away." Then she asked to see a close friend while there was still time. Nothing happened, so Catherine repeated the request, asking if her friend had been sent for. The response was to ignore the request. Why wasn't the friend sent for? An early account of her life explains this lack of sensitivity by excusing it: "Naturally she might wish to see this cherished friend once more, but grace would not allow such gratification to nature." Neither would the acting superior.

Catherine's friendships, which were many and deep, apparently were a cause of concern to some of the sisters, and there may have been strong feelings of jealousy in some of the hearts of those surrounding her deathbed.

Within twenty-five years of Catherine's death, there were 3,000 Sisters of Mercy! And only thirteen years after her death, seven of them disembarked at a growing gold-rush town called San Francisco. How quickly the order spread throughout the world.

Since I wanted to take another look at the grave in which Catherine was buried, I walked out of the room, up a flight of stairs to the rooms that once housed thousands of distressed women and over to a window high in the cloister walls. Down below, I saw a miniature Gothic chapel surrounded by a green lawn. Other than that, there were

119

In Catherine's room

only gray cloister walls everywhere I looked. After doing the sketch of Catherine's grave from the third story window, I walked down to the grave itself. Over it was built an elaborate miniature of this chapel. I wished it were simpler, and I suspect that Catherine, had she a choice, would also have picked something simpler.

Extending out in back and along the side of the miniature chapel was a fine, green-grass plot. All of the early young sisters who had died when the order was first getting started were in that plot. In life as in death, they surrounded Catherine. All of them together gave their lives for true greatness, to follow Jesus Christ in ministering to the poor, the sick and the broken. Together. In life as well as death—and resurrection.

That plot of grass was the most impressive marker I saw in Ireland. Just a green plot, in the center of which was the chapel. Grass, close-cropped, without any markers. I had the feeling I saw a clean valley, filled with grain, where some great battle was fought. Nothing to mark the site—no plaques, no manmade commemorations—just the awareness that years ago this quiet, peaceful site was filled with intense activity.

The contrast between my awareness of the young women buried there, the first whom Catherine gathered around her, and the lack of anything manmade to symbolize their presence, opened up an inner space for me to ponder.

There is an austerity in the Irish character, an austerity born perhaps of having to defend their land and, more precious, their faith. I felt that were this austere streak removed, they would cease to be Irish. This kind of austerity is not easily surrendered. And it shows in the way the Irish love. It certainly showed in the commitment of these young women who died of overwork and exhaustion.

As I entered the building once more, I saw on the wall a list of all the sisters who were buried around Catherine, each individual site carefully marked.

I walked back upstairs to one of the large rooms that had been a classroom, but which now served as a community room for the sisters. Hanging on the wall was a very large picture of Catherine McAuley that served as the model for a stamp issued by the Republic of Ireland in 1978 commemorating her and the Sisters of Mercy. It showed Catherine seated at a small table, her features angular, even stern, yet they seem overly pious at the same time. The picture, which I knew before I had visited Ireland, had always seemed to me to lack vitality—hardly someone I would have called "Kitty," as she often referred to herself when writing to her Sisters:

We sailed from Kingstown . . . arrived at half past six . . . were conducted to the Mersey Hotel . . . laughed and talked over the adventures of the night, particularly my travelling title, changed from your Kitty to friend Catherine, an improvement, you will say.

Sister Finian told me that the picture was painted right after Catherine's death. "At least," she said, "we think it is. You see, we have another picture downstairs in a small room Catherine used as an office sometimes, which might have been the one painted after her death. We're not sure."

I told her I would like to see the other picture. As soon as I did, I was convinced that this second picture was the original painting done after her death. Call it intuition. Sister Finian then surprised me by saying, "What do you think, Father? You're an artist. Which one is the first painted?"

Her question made me approach an answer in a completely new way. Could I, as an artist, tell which was the first one? I tried to visualize the death scene: the body laid out, a handkerchief tying her jaws together so that her mouth wouldn't gape open, the sisters on their knees, praying, candles burning. A scene of sorrow and grief. Then in comes a sister with a large easel and mounts an oversize canvas on it (four by five feet). She primes the huge canvas, charcoals the features on the surface, lays in the base colors—all while the prayers for the dead are being recited. And the painting would require a number of sittings, so to speak. It didn't make any sense. I could not believe a Mercy Sister would have available, in 1841, an easel the size necessary to paint the picture I saw in the community room. No, the picture, if indeed there was one painted right after her death, must have been dashed off in a hurry, and the canvas would

123

The Gothic Miniature

have been smaller, the size the artist could hold in her hand or on her lap.

The second painting was small and bright. It had a freshness and spontaneity about it that could only have come from experiencing the person being painted. Living with a person, and loving her, would account for that fresh quality. There was a directness, a lack of artificiality in that small painting that convinced me it was the one done after her death. Also, its size made it more compatible with the reality of the deathbed scene.

When I told Sister Finian that I thought the original was the smaller of the two paintings, she told me that, as a matter of fact, it was highly insured. It depicted, in my opinion, a real person, someone the artist knew well. I did a sketch from it. Perhaps this was the closet that Catherine mentioned in her letters, a small closet that she retired to in order to write after everyone else had gone to bed, "The fire is out, and the windows are making an awful noise, so I must have done. . ."

Though the fire was out by 1841, the order was only beginning. Within a few years, the Sisters of Mercy were fast becoming the largest order of religious women in the Church. Even as early as 1866 the diversity of their works is surprising: not just poor schools and places for distressed women, not just hospitals, but homes for magdalenes, places of adult instruction, schools for the poor, middle class and for gifted, orphanages, classes for the deaf and blind and homes for the blind and widowed. And all of this went right along with visiting the sick daily.

"The fire is out. . .so I must have done. . ." Still, the woman's spirit lives in 22,000 Sisters of Mercy around the world today, in hundreds of schools, colleges and hospitals.

Catherine McAuley vitally affected the course of medicine, health care and education. In her concern for the poor, she raised to conscious awareness the deepseated and Christian concern for social justice. She gave all that she had for a cause, for a person bigger than herself, Jesus Christ. Once she saw what God wanted of her, she led a full, intense life, a life filled with graciousness, humor and single-hearted dedication to the poor and sick.

She called her life a dance; beneath

the thousand trivialities of the every-day, she saw the underlying rhythm, the dance, as God met man and woman in a warm embrace: the dance of life. She explained this image in a letter to a friend she was to meet in Bermondsey, recalling that she had first to pass through many cities, visiting the new foundations:

I think sometimes our passage through this dear sweet world is something like the dance called "Right and Left." You and I have crossed over, changed places, etc. etc. Your set is finished for a little time, you dance no more, but I have to go through the figure called "Sir Roger de Coverly," too old for your memory. I'll have to curtsie (sic) and bow in Birr presently to change corners going from the one I am in at present to another, take the hands of everyone who does me the honour, and end the figure by coming back to my own place. I'll then have a sea-saw dance to Liverpool and a Merry Jog that has no stop to Birmingham and I hope a second to Bermondsey. When you, Sr. M. Xavier and I will join hands and dance the "Duval Trio" each on the same ground.

We have one solid comfort amidst this little tripping about, our hearts can always be in the same place, centered in God, for whom alone we go forward or stay back. Oh may He look on us with love and pity and then we shall be able to do anything He wishes us to do, no matter how difficult to accomplish.

Pray for your affectionate

M.C. McAuley

127

The Lady from Dublin

Sources

Quotations in the text were taken from the following sources:

History
  1970 Curtis, Edmund. "Ireland in the Early Nineteenth Century." *A History of Ireland.* London: Methuen and Company.

Letters
  1969 *Letters of Catherine McAuley 1827–1841.* Edited (and Introduced) by Sister Ignatia Neuman. R.S.M. Baltimore, Maryland: Helicon Press, Inc.

Life
  1866 *The Life of Catherine McAuley.* By a Member of the Order of Mercy. Montreal, Canada: D. & J. Sadlier and Company.

  1835 McAuley, Catherine. "A Prayer to Seek and Do God's Will." Unpublished prayer from Baggot Street House, Dublin, Ireland.

Records
  1830– "Records of Presentation
  1831 Convent of George's Hill." Dublin, Ireland.

  1950 Savage, Roland, S.J. *Catherine McAuley.* Dublin, Ireland: M.H. Gill and Sons, Ltd.